The Gen X Series

ENGLISH OLYMPIAD 6

Useful for English Olympiads Conducted at School, National & International Levels

Author
Suparna Sengupta

Peer Reviewer
Manasvi Vohra

Strictly According to the Latest Syllabus of English Olympiad

Published by:

F-2/16, Ansari road, Daryaganj, New Delhi-110002
☎ 23240026, 23240027 • *Fax:* 011-23240028
✉ info@vspublishers.com • 🌐 www.vspublishers.com

  Online Brandstore: amazon.in/vspublishers

Regional Office : Hyderabad
5-1-707/1, Brij Bhawan (Beside Central Bank of India Lane)
Bank Street, Koti, Hyderabad - 500 095
☎ 040-24737290
✉ vspublishershyd@gmail.com

Follow us on:

BUY OUR BOOKS FROM: | AMAZON | | FLIPKART |

© Copyright: *V&S PUBLISHERS*
ISBN 978-93-579407-4-0
New Edition

DISCLAIMER

While every attempt has been made to provide accurate and timely information in this book, neither the author nor the publisher assumes any responsibility for errors, unintended omissions or commissions detected therein. The author and publisher makes no representation or warranty with respect to the comprehensiveness or completeness of the contents provided.

All matters included have been simplified under professional guidance for general information only, without any warranty for applicability on an individual. Any mention of an organization or a website in the book, by way of citation or as a source of additional information, doesn't imply the endorsement of the content either by the author or the publisher. It is possible that websites cited may have changed or removed between the time of editing and publishing the book.

Results from using the expert opinion in this book will be totally dependent on individual circumstances and factors beyond the control of the author and the publisher.

It makes sense to elicit advice from well informed sources before implementing the ideas given in the book. The reader assumes full responsibility for the consequences arising out from reading this book.

For proper guidance, it is advisable to read the book under the watchful eyes of parents/guardian. The buyer of this book assumes all responsibility for the use of given materials and information.

The copyright of the entire content of this book rests with the author/publisher. Any infringement/transmission of the cover design, text or illustrations, in any form, by any means, by any entity will invite legal action and be responsible for consequences thereon.

Publisher's Note

General Trade and Mass Appeal books across various genres have helped **V&S Publishers** to gain widespread popularity. In a short span of 10 years, we have successfully published more than 1000 titles across 9 languages in our 50 subject categories. Being into the publishing business for about 40 years, we have always been a dynamic publishing house, with a massive distribution network, across India; including E-commerce platforms.

Understanding the need of inculcating knowledge and developing a spirit of healthy competition amongst students to make them ready for the world outside schools and colleges; we created Olympiad Series under the **GEN X SERIES Imprint** which, owning to its rich content and unique representation became popular amongst students, in no time. The motivation is not to improve marks in terms of numbers, but is to make sure that the students are already prepared to face competitive environment with respect to college admissions and cracking various entrance examinations, while ensuring their conceptual clarity.

Published for classes 1-10 across subjects English, Mathematics, Science, Computers, General Knowledge, the books are unlike any other in the market and are written in a guidebook pattern and exhaustively include examples and Multiple-Choice Questions.

Here, we present the latest Edition of **ENGLISH OLYMPIAD CLASS 6.**

Unique Features of the book are as follows:

- Authored by Subject Matter Experts' and Peer reviewed by School Principals and HOD's for the respective subjects
- Books based on principles of Applied Psychology and Bloom's Taxonomy
- Suited for Olympiad Examinations held at School level, National level & International Level irrespective of organizing body.
- The only Olympiad Book in India written in Guidebook Pattern with Concise Theory, images and illustrations.
- Exhaustively include Examples, MCQs, Subjective Questions, and HOTS with Answer Keys & Solutions.
- Multiple Model Papers for thorough practice also given inside the book with solutions.
- OMR sheets appended at the end of the book for simulating exam environment.

Besides, we are also planning to launch an App very soon for the Olympiad preparation which further testifies our constant endeavor to keep up with student demands. We have made sure to closely follow syllabus patterns of not only Olympiad conducting bodies but also education boards & organizations like CBSE and NCERT, to make sure that our books prove useful to students; helping them to boost their academic performance in schools as well.

P.S. While every care has been taken to ensure the correctness of the content, if you come across any error, howsoever minor, do not hesitate to discuss with teachers while pointing that out to us in no uncertain terms.

We wish you All the Best!

DISTINCTIVE

WHY OLYMPIADS?

Olympiads are just like competitive exams; conducted by various bodies at national and international levels. The aim is to experience a competitive examination at the school level and also to help students to discover their interest acrss subjects like English, Mathematics, Science and General Knowledge.

WHY V&S OLYMPIADS?

We at V&S Publishers aim to build an avid-reading student audience. Hence, our resolve is to follow an innovative pedagogic pattern which would help students to navigate through the book with utmost ease and comfort. Crisp theory practical examples and illustrations keep our book interactive and comprehensive.

01 LEARNING OBJECTIVES
They list the whole chapter as subtopics, helping the teachers to guide children in a step-by-step manner.

02 DID YOU KNOW
Enhance your knowledge by getting acquainted with some amazing facts across various subjects like science, Mathematics and English.

03 MULTIPLE CHOICE QUESTIONS
MCQs act as an excellent learning aid, helping you to understand and work on your mistakes.

04 THINGS TO REMEMBER
A quick recap of the chapter in a summarized format helps in faster revision along with conceptual clarity.

05 HOTS
The High Order Thinking Questions aim to help the student to solve Application-based questions and gain practical understanding of the subject.

FEATURES

06 SUBJECTIVE QUESTIONS
Help to place the knowledge gained in orderly fashion by using "WH" questions, mostly in the form of bullet points.

07 ACHIEVER'S SECTION
Offers a quick revision of the book along with some new facts for the students to discover.

08 A SET OF OMR SHEETS
To allow the student to practice question in an exam-like format which would help them to get the "feel" of how Olympiad exams take place.

09 MODEL TEST PAPERS
Two model test papers are provided at the end of each book, which help the student to test the knowledge which they have gained after thorough reading of all chapters.

10 ANSWER KEY & SOLUTIONS
Detailed Answer Key along with explanations aid the pupil to indentify, understand the mistakes they make during the course of Olympiad preparation.

COMPLEMENT SCHOOL SYLLABI

The syllabi across all Olympiad examination closely follow the pattern of academic books. Hence, they not only provide a competitive examination experience, but also help to revise topics for school examinations as well, while strengthening conceptual precision.

ENHANCEMENT OF ANALYTICAL & LOGICAL REASONING

Practicing analytical ability questions, not only helps in developing intellectual ability but also plays a vital role in building critical thinking ability which helps an individual to think about a question or a crisis like situation in day to day life; from all aspects and directions.

Note to Parents

Dear Parents,

Olympiad examinations come with a plethora of advantages. First and foremost among such advantages is the application of knowledge studied, in the form of multiple-choice questions. It helps the child not only to step away from rote learning, but also helps them to exhibit their competencies across various subjects.

In addition to this, Olympiads help the student to understand the importance of revision and practice, and to imbibe upon these practices; which also prove useful in academic performance of the child.

The Olympiads are conducted across multiple subjects, and help the child to recognize their field of interest, thereby encouraging the students to make a career in the field where they can excel the most.

However, cognitive development of a child is not just limited to the four walls of classroom. Following steps can be encouraged by you, to ensure their ward is able to grasp various concepts with ease or lesser difficulty:

- **Eat a balanced diet:** Ensure intake of vitamins and minerals to keep you active. Include fruits and super foods like millet in your diet to ensure healthy functioning of organs. Huge intake of junk food should be avoided.
- **Indulge in outdoor activities:** Outdoor games break the monotony of life. Play your heart out in greenery to keep yourself alert, active and fit.
- **Sleep well:** A sound sleep of 7-8 hours refreshes the brain and makes it ready to understand new topics with more clarity. A sleep derived person faces difficulty in doing even the simplest tasks of day to day life.
- **Reduce your Screen time:** More screen time leads to not only weakening of eyesight but decreases concentration span. Regulated Screen time should be encouraged
- **Do not hesitate to raise a hand:** Having a doubt in class? Do not hesitate to ask your parents or teachers. This ensures more Conceptual Clarity and hence leads to Application based understanding of various subjects and topics.
- **Teach and Learn:** No need to do rote-learning. Once you understand a topic teach or explain it to your friends, siblings and parents. It brings clarity and ensures the child does his revision this way.
- **Keep smiling:** A positive attitude promotes a growth mindset and encourages the child to be more inquisitive and try to learn something new, everyday!

HAPPY LEARNING!

Contents

SECTION 1: WORD AND STRUCTURE KNOWLEDGE

1. Nouns — 9
2. Pronouns — 13
3. Adjectives — 19
4. Articles — 23
5. Verbs — 27
6. Adverbs — 33
7. Prepositions — 38
8. Conjunctions — 44
9. Phrasal Verbs — 48
10. Punctuations — 53
11. Tenses — 57
12. Voice — 61
13. Narration — 67
14. Spellings — 74
15. Collocation — 78
16. Idioms — 83
17. Vocabulary — 89

SECTION 2: READING COMPREHENSION

Reading Comprehension — 93

SECTION 3: SPOKEN AND WRITTEN EXPRESSIONS

Agreements and Disagreements, Requests, and Refusals — 109

SECTION 4: ACHIEVERS' SECTION

Some Thoughtful Question — 114
Subjective Section — 118
Model Test Paper–1 — 125
Model Test Paper–2 — 128

ANSWER KEYS (Access Content online on Dropbox) — 132
Appendix — 146

SECTION 1
WORD AND STRUCTURE KNOWLEDGE

Nouns

Learning Objectives: In this chapter, students will learn about:
- Kinds of Noun
- Uses of Nouns

CHAPTER SUMMARY

A noun is a naming word which identifies a person, a place, an animal, a thing, an idea or a feeling in a sentence.

Examples:
John, Jupiter, Singapore, elephant, book, teacher, man, girl, pencil, freedom, happiness etc.

Kinds of Noun

Proper Noun
Proper nouns name particular persons, places or things. They are the names of individual entities and begin with capital letters.

Examples:
Barack Obama, China, Sunday, Chicago etc.

Common Noun
Common nouns refer to general things. They are the common names given to persons or things of same kind or class.

Examples:
girl, doctor, animals, jaguars, flowers, country, shop, month, ship etc.

Collective Noun
Collective nouns refer to a collection of things spoken of as a whole.

Examples:
flock, family, audience, herd, army etc.

Abstract Noun
Abstract nouns refer to ideas, feelings, quality or concepts. We cannot see, touch, taste and smell these nouns.

Examples:
love, beauty, courage, poverty, hunger, sweetness etc.

Uses of Noun

- **Subject of the sentence:** The subject is the person, place, thing, or idea that the sentence is about.

  Example:
  The book is very useful.

- **Direct object of a verb:** The direct object is the person, place, thing, or idea, that receives the action of the verb.

  Example:
  Rohan slammed the door.

- **Indirect object of a verb:** The indirect object receives the action of the verb indirectly.

  Example: Our teacher gave us a prize.

- **Object of a preposition:** A preposition is a word that shows location, movement, or direction. Common prepositons are in, on, with, under for, and by. A preposition is always followed by a noun or pronoun that is called the object of the preposition. Together, they form a prepositional phrase.

  Example:
  over the house
  under the bridge

> **TRIVIA**
>
> A pangram sentence is one that contains every letter in the language. The quick brown fox jumps over the lazy dog

- **Object complement:** An object complement is a word that completes the meaning of a direct object. It is used when the direct object would not make complete sense by itself.

    Example:
    I named my cat, Pussy.

- **To show possession:** A possessive noun tells who or what owns something.

    Example:
    Hawaii's volcanoes are still active.

- **Predicate noun:** A predicate noun comes after the verb to be or a linking verb that replaces or means the same thing as the subject of the sentence.

    Example:
    My brother is the clown. (Clown is the predicate noun)

- **Appositive:** An appositive is a word or phrase that comes after another word. It explains, identifies, or gives information about that word. The appositive is set off from the sentence by one or two commas.

    Example:
    Our teacher, Mr. Sharma, taught us English.

MUST REMEMBER

➡ A noun is a naming word which identifies a person, a place, an animal, a thing, an idea or a feeling in a sentence.

➡ Collective nouns refer to a collection of things spoken of as a whole.

➡ Abstract nouns refer to ideas, feelings, quality or concepts.

➡ The subject is the person, place, thing, or idea that the sentence is about.

➡ An object complement is a word that completes the meaning of a direct object.v

PRACTICE EXERCISE

I. Identify the type of underlined noun(s) in the following sentences and choose the correct option.

1. The <u>plane</u> landed safely at the airport.
   (a) Proper (b) Common
   (c) Collective (d) Abstract
2. The <u>paper</u> packages were tied up with strings.
   (a) Proper (b) Common
   (c) Collective (d) Abstract
3. <u>Sundarbans</u> is a vast swamp.
   (a) Proper (b) Common
   (c) Collective (d) Abstract
4. Our <u>class</u> consists of forty students.
   (a) Proper (b) Common
   (c) Collective (d) Abstract
5. She recognized him by his <u>name</u>.
   (a) Proper (b) Common
   (c) Collective (d) Abstract
6. <u>Honesty</u> is the best policy.
   (a) Proper (b) Common
   (c) Collective (d) Abstract
7. My <u>parents</u> went on a vacation to Las Vegas.
   (a) Proper (b) Common
   (c) Collective (d) Abstract
8. <u>Apples</u> are delicious.
   (a) Proper (b) Common
   (c) Collective (d) Abstract
9. <u>Zebras</u> and <u>tigers</u> have stripes.
   (a) Proper (b) Common
   (c) Collective (d) Abstract
10. <u>Dogs</u> love their families.
    (a) Proper (b) Common
    (c) Collective (d) Abstract
11. <u>Cheetahs</u> are man-eating animals.
    (a) Proper (b) Common
    (c) Collective (d) Abstract
12. <u>Jason</u> spent more time on Maths.
    (a) Proper (b) Common
    (c) Collective (d) Abstract
13. I don't have much <u>luggage</u>.
    (a) Proper (b) Common
    (c) Collective (d) Abstract
14. There is room for everyone to sit down; there are a lot of <u>chairs</u>.
    (a) Proper (b) Common
    (c) Collective (d) Abstract
15. The <u>lioness</u> gave birth to a litter of cubs.
    (a) Proper (b) Common
    (c) Collective (d) Abstract

II. Identify the type of the underlined noun and choose the correct option.

1. Potato chips are my favourite <u>snack</u>.
   (a) Proper (b) Common
   (c) Collective (d) Abstract
2. Have you been to the <u>Disney World</u>?
   (a) Proper (b) Common
   (c) Collective (d) Abstract
3. The museum is closed on <u>Sunday</u>.
   (a) Proper (b) Common
   (c) Collective (d) Abstract
4. The dog is a <u>faithful</u> animal.
   (a) Proper (b) Common
   (c) Collective (d) Abstract
5. A <u>herd of cattle</u> was blocking the way.
   (a) Proper (b) Common
   (c) Collective (d) Abstract
6. I borrowed two books from the <u>library</u>.
   (a) Proper (b) Common
   (c) Collective (d) Abstract
7. I forgot to carry <u>my pack of cards</u> with me.
   (a) Proper (b) Common
   (c) Collective (d) Abstract
8. In some countries, people are still not <u>free</u>.
   (a) Proper (b) Common
   (c) Collective (d) Abstract
9. The <u>Earth</u> is a planet.
   (a) Proper (b) Common
   (c) Collective (d) Abstract
10. You must always speak the <u>truth</u>.
    (a) Proper (b) Common
    (c) Collective (d) Abstract
11. The young <u>lad</u> did not know what to say.
    (a) Proper (b) Common
    (c) Collective (d) Abstract

12. Forrest Gump is my favourite movie.
    (a) Proper   (b) Common
    (c) Collective   (d) Abstract
13. Dave caught a fish with a hook.
    (a) Proper   (b) Common
    (c) Collective   (d) Abstract
14. Health is more important than wealth.
    (a) Proper   (b) Common
    (c) Collective   (d) Abstract
15. He is good at telling funny stories.
    (a) Proper   (b) Common
    (c) Collective   (d) Abstract

III. Fill in the blanks with suitable noun from the given options.

1. He had to pay for his _____.
    (a) foolishness   (b) selfish
    (c) brave   (d) heart
2. The _____ is the father of man.
    (a) father   (b) sister
    (c) child   (d) mother
3. The doctor kept his _____ waiting for long before seeing them.
    (a) patients   (b) singers
    (c) waiters   (d) dancers
4. We did not have any wooden _____ when we moved to our new house.
    (a) shoes   (b) clothes
    (c) furniture   (d) cutlery
5. The _____ of this story is a brave man and has a great personality.
    (a) heroine   (b) hero
    (c) villain   (d) reader
6. Are you _____ that you will pass the test?
    (a) confident   (b) failed
    (c) sad   (d) angry
7. I have brown hair, but my sister's _____ is black.
    (a) skin   (b) hair
    (c) teeth   (d) dress
8. The World Cup win was a _____ moment for the entire country.
    (a) unhappy   (b) bad
    (c) proud   (d) shameful
9. He bought a beautiful chestnut _____ to add to his animal farm.
    (a) horse   (b) chair
    (c) car   (d) table
10. I have lost my _____ of keys.
    (a) house   (b) bunch
    (c) number   (d) door

HOTS

I. Select the option that identifies noun in the following sentences.

1. Mr. Dass, have you met your new boss?
    (a) Have   (b) Met
    (c) Your   (d) Boss
2. Her parents tried living in the north, but they could not adapt to the cold.
    (a) North   (b) But
    (c) Not   (d) Adapt
3. Mastering basic mathematics is an important goal for younger students.
    (a) Mastering   (b) Important
    (c) Younger   (d) Students
4. To seize a foreign embassy and its inhabitants is flagrant disregard for diplomatic neutrality.
    (a) Seize   (b) Its
    (c) Flagrant   (d) Neutrality
5. The Trojans' rash decision to accept the wooden horse led to their destruction.
    (a) Their   (b) Led
    (c) Accept   (d) Destruction

II.
1. Choose a noun that does not belong to the group:
    (a) Building   (b) City
    (c) Mount Everest   (d) Country
2. Choose a noun that does not belong to the group:
    (a) Bundle   (b) Flock
    (c) Crowd   (d) Bird
3. Choose a noun that does not belong to the group:
    (a) Beauty   (b) Ink
    (c) Wood   (d) Stone

Mark the noun for the home of the given animal:
4. A _____ of an alligator.
    (a) hole   (b) nest
    (c) lodge   (d) coop
5. A _____ of a rabbit.
    (a) pen   (b) den
    (c) kennel   (d) burrow

Pronouns

Learning Objectives: In this chapter, students will learn about:
- ✓ Basics of Pronoun
- ✓ Kinds of Pronoun
- ✓ Uses of Pronoun

CHAPTER SUMMARY

Pronouns are words that are used in place of nouns. They refer to previously mentioned nouns. We use pronouns to avoid the repetition of nouns.
Example:
Jessica's father asked Jessica to bring Jessica's father a pen. (Incorrect)
Jessica's father asked **her** to bring **him** a pen. (Correct)
We can avoid repetition of the noun Jessica by using pronouns 'her' and 'him'.

Kinds of Pronouns

Personal Pronouns
Personal pronouns refer to the speaker, the person spoken to and the person spoken about. They are used when we do not want to mention the name of a person or thing more than once.
Examples:
Parul is a close friend. Parul is from Delhi.
Parul is a close friend. **She** is from Delhi.
Sam loves being in India. Sam does not want to leave.
Sam loves being in India. He does not want to leave.

Personal pronouns include:
- Pronouns of 1st person.
  Examples: I, Me, My, Mine, We, Our, Us
- Pronouns of 2nd person.
  Examples: You, Your, Yours
- Pronouns of 3rd person
  Examples: He, She, It, They, Theirs, Them

Possessive Pronouns
Possessive pronouns indicate possession or the relationship of a person or thing to another person or thing.
Examples:
This book is **mine**.
('Mine' describes the relationship between the book and its owner.)
I have lost my pen. May I use **yours**?
('Yours' suggests possession on the pen by a person.)

Possessive pronouns include:

mine	yours	hers
ours	theirs	his

Reflexive Pronouns
Reflexive pronoun lays emphasis on the same person or thing in a sentence. It is a special form of personal pronoun.
Examples:
He **himself** said so.
I looked at **myself** in the mirror.

Relative Pronouns
Relative pronouns are used to join two sentences.
Example:
The boy **who** is singing is my friend. (A boy is singing. He is my friend.)
The car **which** I like is red.
The man **whom** I met yesterday is a magician. (Here the words shown in bold are relative pronouns.)

Relative pronouns include:

| who | whose | which | whom | that |

Demonstrative Pronoun
Demonstrative pronouns point to a particular thing or things.

Examples:
This is my desk.
That is his choice.
These socks are mine. **Those** are his shoes.

Uses of Pronouns
The following are a few uses of pronouns. There are three main uses of pronouns: subject (he) object (him), or possessive (his).

- Subject pronouns are used when the pronoun is the subject of the sentence. You can learn subject pronouns easily by filling in the blank subject space in a simple sentence.
  Example:
  ___ did the job. (who did the job?)
  I, he, she, we, they, who, whoever can be used as subject pronouns.

- Subject pronouns are also used if they rename the subject. They follow verbs *to be* such as is, are, was, were, am, will be, had been, etc.
  Examples:
  It is he.
  This is she speaking.
  It is we who are responsible for the decision.

  Note: In informal English, most people tend to follow verbs *to be* with object pronouns like me, her, them.
  Examples:
  It could have been them.
  It could have been they. (Grammatically correct)
  It is just me at the door.
  It is just I at the door. (Grammatically correct)

- When *who* refers to a personal pronoun (I, you, he, she, we, they), it takes the verb that agrees with that pronoun.
  Examples:
  It is I who am sorry. (**Correct**)
  It is I who is sorry. (**Incorrect**)
  It is you who are mistaken. (**Correct**)
  It is you who's mistaken. (**Incorrect**)

- There are object pronouns, known more specifically as direct object, indirect object, and object of a preposition. Object pronouns include me, him, herself, us, them, themselves.
  Examples:
  Jean saw him.
  (*Him* is the direct object of the verb *saw*.)
  Raman gives her the book.
  The direct object of the verb *give* is book, and her is the indirect object. Indirect objects always have an implied to or for in front of them: Give [to] her the book. Do [for] me a favour.
  Are you talking to me?
  (Me is the object of the preposition *to*.)

- The pronouns who, that, and which become singular or plural depending on the subject. If the subject is singular, use a singular verb. If it is plural, use a plural verb.
  Examples:
  He is the only one of those men who is always on time.
  (The word who refers to one. Therefore, use the singular verb is.)
  Sometimes we must look more closely to find true subject of a verb:
  He is one of those men who are always on time.
  (The word who refers to men. Therefore, use the plural verb are.)

- Pronouns that are singular (I, he, she, everyone, everybody, anyone, anybody, no one, nobody, someone, somebody, each, either, neither, etc.) require singular verbs. This rule is frequently overlooked when using the pronouns each, either, and neither, followed by of. Those three pronouns always take singular verbs.
  Examples:
  Each of the girls sings well.
  Either of us is capable of doing the job.
  Neither of them is available to speak right now.

Exception:

When each follows a noun or pronoun in certain sentences, even experienced writers sometimes do mistakes:

Examples:

The women each gave her approval. (**Incorrect**)

The women each gave their approval. (**Correct**)

The words, are and there, each ends with a silent vowel. (**Incorrect**)

The words, are and there, each end with a silent vowel. (**Correct**)

These examples do not contradict above use because each is not the subject, but rather an adjunct describing the true subject.

- To decide whether to use the subject or object pronoun after the words *than* or *as*, depends on the sense. But the subject pronouns are preferred.

   Example:

   Sonali is as smart as she/her.

   (Here it will be correct to say Sonali is as smart as she is. Therefore, she is the correct answer.)

   Example:

   Zoe is taller than I/me.

   (Here it will correct to say that Zoe is taller than I am.)

- The possessive pronouns yours, his, hers, its, ours, theirs, and whose never need apostrophes. Avoid mistakes like her's and your's.

- The only time it's has an apostrophe is when it is a contraction for it is or it has.

- The only time who's has an apostrophe is when it means who is or who has.

- There is no apostrophe in oneself. Avoid 'one's self,' a common error.

   Examples:

   It's been a cold morning.

   He's the one who's always on time.

   He's the one whose wife is always on time.

   Keeping oneself ready is important.

- Pronouns that end in -self or -selves are called reflexive pronouns. There are nine reflexive pronouns: myself, yourself, himself, herself, itself, oneself, ourselves, yourselves, and themselves.

Reflexive pronouns are used when both the subject and the object of a verb are the same person or thing.

Examples:

Joe helped himself.

- If the object of a preposition refers to a previous noun or pronoun, use a reflexive pronoun:

   Example:

   Joe bought it for himself.

- Reflexive pronouns help avoid confusion. Without them, we might be stuck with sentences like Joe helped Joe.

   Example:

   My brother and myself did it. (Incorrect)

   My brother and I did it. (Correct)

   (Don't use myself unless the pronoun I or me precedes it in the sentence.)

   Please, give it to John or myself. (Incorrect)

   Please, give it to John or me. (Correct)

   You saw me being myself. (Correct)

   (Myself refers back to me in the act of being.

- A sentence like 'Help yourself.' looks like an exception to the rule until we realize it's shorthand for '*You may help yourself*'. In certain cases, a reflexive pronoun may come first.)

   Example:

   Doubting himself, the man proceeded cautiously.

- Reflexive pronouns are also used for emphasis.

   Example:

   He himself finished the whole job.

- The use of they and their with singular pronouns is not considered good by many authors. To be consistent, it is a good practice to avoid they and its variants (e.g., them, their, themselves) with previously singular nouns or pronouns.

   Examples:

   Someone has to do it, and they have to do it well. (Not consistent)

   Someone has to do it, and he or she has to do it well. (Grammatically correct)

   Someone has to do it, and has to do it well. (Rewritten)

(The problem is that someone is singular, but they is plural. If we change they to he or she, we get a rather clumsy sentence, even if it is technically correct. The better option is to rewrite the sentence.)

TRIVIA

'Supercalifragilisticexpialidocious' (*Breath*) is not the longest word in English.

- Following are more examples of why rewriting is a better idea than using he or she or him or her to keep sentences consistent.

Examples:

No one realizes when their time is up. (Inconsistent)

No one realizes when his or her time is up. (Awkward)

None realize when their time is up. (Rewritten)

If you see anyone on the trail, tell them to be careful. (Inconsistent)

If you see anyone on the trail, tell him or her to be careful. (Awkward)

Tell anyone you see on the trail to be careful. (Rewritten)

- When a pronoun is joined with antoher noun by and use the pronoun of proper case, subjective, objective, or possessive.

Examples:

Her and her friend came over. (Incorrect)

She and her friend came over. (Correct)

(If we remove *and her friend*, we're left with the ungrammatical *Her came over.*)

I invited he and his wife. (Incorrect)

I invited him and his wife. (Correct)

(If we remove *and his wife*, we're left with the ungrammatical *I invited he.*)

Bill asked my sister and I. (Incorrect)

Bill asked my sister and me. (Correct)

(If we remove *my sister and*, we're left with the ungrammatical *Bill asked I.*)

MUST REMEMBER

➡ Pronouns are words that are used in place of nouns.
➡ Personal pronouns refer to the speaker, the person spoken to and the person spoken about.
➡ Possessive pronouns indicate possession or the relationship of a person or thing to another person or thing.
➡ Subject pronouns are used when the pronoun is the subject of the sentence.
➡ Pronouns that end in -self or -selves are called reflexive pronouns.

PRACTICE EXERCISE

I. Identify the type of the underlined pronouns and choose the correct option.

1. <u>She</u> has gone to school.
   (a) Personal (b) Possessive
   (c) Relative (d) Reflexive

2. Let me introduce <u>myself</u>. My name is Alan.
   (a) Personal (b) Possessive
   (c) Relative (d) Reflexive

3. We need an umbrella. Can you lend us <u>yours</u>?
   (a) Personal (b) Possessive
   (c) Relative (d) Reflexive

4. <u>You</u> should be blamed for the mistake.
   (a) Personal (b) Possessive
   (c) Relative (d) Reflexive

5. We contributed our share. They have contributed <u>theirs</u>.
   (a) Personal (b) Possessive
   (c) Relative (d) Reflexive

6. They <u>themselves</u> revealed the truth.
   (a) Personal (b) Possessive
   (c) Relative (d) Reflexive

7. This is the girl <u>who</u> spoke to us just now.
   (a) Personal (b) Relative
   (c) Possessive (d) Reflexive

8. The book <u>which</u> you just bought at the store is a bestseller.
   (a) Personal (b) Relative
   (c) Possessive (d) Reflexive

9. The baby got up <u>himself</u> after falling down.
   (a) Personal (b) Relative
   (c) Reflexive (d) Possessive

10. They were looking for a charger. I really don't want to give <u>mine</u> to anyone.
    (a) Personal (b) Relative
    (c) Possessive (d) Reflexive

11. <u>She</u> prepared the food.
    (a) Personal (b) Relative
    (c) Possessive (d) Reflexive

12. We live in an apartment. <u>Theirs</u> is an old-fashioned mansion.
    (a) Personal (b) Relative
    (c) Possessive (d) Reflexive

13. Those pet cats are <u>ours</u>.
    (a) Personal (b) Relative
    (c) Possessive (d) Reflexive

14. <u>You</u> are an angel.
    (a) Personal (b) Relative
    (c) Possessive (d) Reflexive

15. <u>They</u> are preparing for the examination.
    (a) Personal (b) Relative
    (c) Possessive (d) Reflexive

II. Choose the correct option to replace the words given in bold.

1. Are these your books? They are not **my books**.
   (a) mine (b) ours
   (c) yours (d) theirs

2. This is Megha. **Megha** is in my class.
   (a) he (b) she
   (c) her (d) his

3. My uncle asked me how I managed to find **my uncle's** house.
   (a) he (b) she
   (c) her (d) his

4. The speaker used difficult language. No one understood what **the speaker** said
   (a) he (b) she
   (c) her (d) his

5. I shall mind my business. He should mind my **business**.
   (a) he (b) she
   (c) her (d) his

6. Teddy's house is right next to **my house**.
   (a) theirs (b) mine
   (c) her (d) his

7. After Jess got a bad report card, **Jess** wanted to hide it from **Jess's** parents.
   (a) he/his (b) she/him
   (c) her/she (d) his/him

8. The team is hoping **the team** will regain some of the points they lost in the first round
   (a) he (b) she
   (c) them (d) they

9. Although Riya started last, **Riya's** was the best looking painting of all.
   (a) he (b) she
   (c) hers (d) his

10. My clothes were still a little wet when I took **my clothes** out of the dryer.
    (a) them (b) they
    (c) her (d) his

III. **Choose the correct option to fill in the blanks.**

1. I like to read at night when _____ go to bed
   (a) I (b) me
   (c) myself (d) mine

2. My little sister made a mud pie for _____.
   (a) I (b) me
   (c) myself (d) mine

3. Our football coach told _____ to get plenty of sleep.
   (a) I (b) me
   (c) us (d) we

4. _____ tried to hail a taxi, but had no luck.
   (a) We (b) Us
   (c) Them (d) Me

5. The last family to hike down the mountain was _____.
   (a) their (b) theirs
   (c) they (d) there's

6. _____ face began to droop when he knew he couldn't go out.
   (a) He (b) Him
   (c) His (d) Her

7. When the sailor came home from the war, his family was there to greet _____.
   (a) him (b) he
   (c) his (d) her

8. We had to release our bird because _____ was not eating properly in captivity.
   (a) her (b) she
   (c) herself (d) hers

9. Everyone wants to get _____ own way.
   (a) their (b) theirs
   (c) they (d) there's

10. Her parents were in Malaysia. So were _____.
    (a) me (b) my
    (c) mine (d) theirs

11. You must not blame _____. You are the one at fault.
    (a) my (b) I
    (c) mine (d) me

12. After such a wonderful performance, _____ wanted to applaud loudly.
    (a) we (b) us
    (c) them (d) our

13. I did not intend to hurt _____ feelings, so I apologized to her.
    (a) his (b) her
    (c) she (d) him

14. We had to buy a new radio because _____ stopped working.
    (a) our (b) ours
    (c) we (d) us

15. _____ job is it to sweep the floor?
    (a) Who (b) Who's
    (c) Whose (d) Whom

HOTS

1. Identify the sentences in the following questions where pronouns are not needed.
   (a) This is my bag.
   (b) You and I have done our duty.
   (c) One should do ones duty.
   (d) The slave hid himself in a cave.

2. Identify the sentences in the following questions where pronouns are not needed.
   (a) The jury gave its verdict.
   (b) She qualified herself as a doctor.
   (c) They love each other.
   (d) Each will go his own way.

3. Identify the sentences in the following questions where pronouns are not needed.
   (a) Every teacher and every student should do his duty himself.
   (b) That house is ours.
   (c) Give your letter to me.
   (d) I and you have broken this table.

4. Yesterday we entered __I__ new house. It is small but it has all the amenities __II__ a man can dream of. __III__ have named our new house 'The Nest'. Constructing a house is not easy. First, __IV__ has to choose the location then the building plan and then the construction is to be supervised with one's own eyes.

   I. (a) mine (b) our
      (c) his (d) him
   II. (a) what (b) which
       (c) that (d) his
   III. (a) His (b) Him
        (c) We (d) Ours
   IV. (a) oneself (b) our self
       (c) myself (d) one

International English Olympiad – 6

Adjectives

Learning Objectives : In this chapter, students will learn about:
- Basics of Adjectives
- Kinds of Adjectives

CHAPTER SUMMARY

Adjectives are words that describe or modify other words, usually nouns. They can identify or quantify another person or thing in a sentence. Adjectives are usually positioned before the noun or pronoun that they modify.

Examples:

We were standing next to a **tall** tree.

It was a **cold** morning.

The **shortest** man won the race.

I am **happy**, but they are **sad**.

Here, the words shown in bold are adjectives.

Kinds of Adjectives

Descriptive Adjectives

Descriptive adjectives describe nouns: they tell us about its colour, size, shape, condition, etc. These adjectives are the most common types of adjectives.

Examples:

dangerous criminals, **green** vegetables, a **square** box, a **big** house, a **funny** story

The words shown in bold are descriptive adjectives.

Quantitative Adjectives

Quantitative adjectives tell us the number (how many) or amount (how much) of a noun.

Examples:

He has eaten **three** apples.

I don't have **much** money.

A little learning is a dangerous thing.

This long and thin centipede has **many** legs.

The words shown in bold are quantitative adjectives.

TRIVIA

The shortest, oldest, and most commonly used word is 'I'.

Demonstrative Adjectives

Demonstrative adjectives are used to point out facts or indicate a particular noun or pronoun. They include 'this', 'that', 'these' and 'those'.

Examples:

This red balloon is mine.

That cute baby is his brother.

These two cats have stripes on their bodies.

I really like **those** shoes.

The words shown in bold are demonstrative adjectives.

Possessive Adjectives

Possessive adjectives express possession of a noun by someone or something. They include 'my', 'her', 'his', 'her', 'its', 'our' and 'their'.

Examples:

Her essay was considered the best.

This is **our** plan.

The words shown in bold are possessive adjectives.

Attributive and Predicative Adjectives

Most adjectives can be used in two positions.

1. When they are used before the noun they describe, and are called attributive adjectives.

Example:
a *black* cat
a *gloomy* outlook

2. When adjectives are used after a verb such as be, become, grow, look, or seem, they're called predicative adjectives.

Examples:
The cat was *black*.
The future looks *gloomy*.

Some adjectives be used in both positions.
For example, the following sentences are grammatically correct:

- She was alone that evening. [alone = predicative]
- It was a mere scratch. [mere = attributive]

MUST REMEMBER

- Adjectives are usually positioned before the noun or pronoun that they modify.
- Descriptive adjectives describe nouns: they tell us about its colour, size, shape, condition, etc.
- Quantitative adjectives tell us the number (how many) or amount (how much) of a noun.
- Demonstrative adjectives are used to point out facts or indicate a particular noun or pronoun.
- Possessive adjectives express possession of a noun by someone or something.

PRACTICE EXERCISE

I. Identify adjectives in the following sentences and choose the correct option.

1. Surprised and excited, Vanessa screamed with happiness when she found her dog.
   (a) Vanessa, dog
   (b) She, her
   (c) Screamed, found
   (d) Surprised, excited

2. The police have found the missing boy.
   (a) missing   (b) police
   (c) found   (d) have

3. Although it was a cold morning, he did not wear his sweater.
   (a) Although   (b) morning
   (c) cold   (d) sweater

4. Aryan lifted the cylindrical beam in the gym.
   (a) cylindrical   (b) gym
   (c) lifted   (d) beam

5. The big, black dog chased the tall man.
   (a) big, black, tall   (b) big, black, dog
   (c) tall   (d) chased

II. Choose the correct descriptive adjectives and fill in the blanks.

1. He was so _____ that he fell asleep as soon as he lay on his bed.
   (a) amused   (b) frightened
   (c) tired   (d) clever

2. This sum is too _____ for me to solve.
   (a) difficult   (b) easy
   (c) many   (d) simple

3. All the students felt _____ as the teacher was about to announce the results.
   (a) relieved   (b) anxious
   (c) angry   (d) sorry

4. Everyone applauded Tejas for his _____ act.
   (a) bad   (b) mischief
   (c) terrible   (d) brave

5. The sky is turning _____ and it seems like it is going to rain.
   (a) red   (b) clear
   (c) dark   (d) yellow

6. The language of this book is _____ to understand than that one.
   (a) easy   (b) English
   (c) written   (d) French

7. Use your keys to open the _____ door.
   (a) unlocked   (b) locked
   (c) broken   (d) sealed

8. The slope is too _____, you cannot run up it.
   (a) deserted   (b) smooth
   (c) steep   (d) gentle

9. This river hasn't been cleaned since long time. It is very _____.
   (a) muddy   (b) crystal clear
   (c) blue   (d) cold

10. It was _____ of you to offer them help.
    (a) selfish   (b) horrible
    (c) cruel   (d) kind

11. I have been feeling _____ lately and have not felt like doing anything.
    (a) energetic   (b) lazy
    (c) active   (d) excited

12. Neither Andrew nor Janet likes to talk in front of a _____ group.
    (a) stupid   (b) clever
    (c) big   (d) small

13. He draws a _____ salary and leads a _____ life.
    (a) poor, luxurious   (b) huge, luxurious
    (c) huge, poor   (d) poor, poor

14. The neighbour's dog was too ____, it would not stop barking at us.
    (a) lovely   (b) friendly
    (c) disciplined (d) annoying

15. Kevin is _____ because he is going to be a father soon.
    (a) excited   (b) unhappy
    (c) disturbed   (d) heartbroken

III. Find out the type of adjectives of the underlined words and choose the correct option.

1. <u>Seven</u> students did not qualify for the boards.
   (a) Descriptive   (b) Quantitative
   (c) Demonstrative (d) Possessive

2. The bark is the <u>external</u> covering of a tree.
   (a) Descriptive   (b) Quantitative
   (c) Demonstrative (d) Possessive

Adjectives

3. Try using <u>this</u> paintbrush in the art class.
   (a) Descriptive (b) Quantitative
   (c) Demonstrative (d) Possessive
4. Why didn't you clean <u>your</u> room?
   (a) Descriptive (b) Quantitative
   (c) Demonstrative (d) Possessive
5. The chameleon can change <u>its</u> color.
   (a) Descriptive (b) Quantitative
   (c) Demonstrative (d) Possessive
6. <u>These</u> flowers smell nice.
   (a) Descriptive (b) Quantitative
   (c) Demonstrative (d) Possessive
7. She ate the <u>whole</u> apple.
   (a) Descriptive (b) Quantitative
   (c) Demonstrative (d) Possessive
8. The <u>helpful</u> teacher was concerned about the students' weaknesses.
   (a) Descriptive (b) Quantitative
   (c) Demonstrative (d) Possessive
9. He lost <u>all</u> his wealth.
   (a) Descriptive (b) Quantitative
   (c) Demonstrative (d) Possessive
10. My house is <u>big</u>. It's got five bedrooms.
    (a) Descriptive (b) Quantitative
    (c) Demonstrative (d) Possessive

HOTS

Choose the correct adjectival phrase from the options given below:

1. The postman _____ came this morning with a parcel for my mother.
   (a) in his smart uniform
   (b) smart uniformed
   (c) smart uniform
   (d) with his smart uniform
2. While I was walking in the garden, I saw a _____ butterfly.
   (a) coloured brightly
   (b) brightly coloured
   (c) bright colours
   (d) brightly colour
3. I'd like a jar of _____ jam, please.
   (a) home make
   (b) home making
   (c) home-made
   (d) made home
4. Find out the Adjectives from the following sentences. It is the world's largest group of islands forming a ten thousand islands chain.
   (a) It is the
   (b) world's largest
   (c) group of islands
   (d) a ten thousand islands
5. Find out the Adjectives from the following sentences. Some property of lead is its softness and resistance.
   (a) some property
   (b) lead are
   (c) softness and resistance
   (d) and resistance

Articles

Learning Objectives : In this chapter, students will learn about:
- ✓ Kind of Articles
- ✓ Use of Articles

CHAPTER SUMMARY

Articles are words that are used before nouns. The words – a, an, the – are called articles.

Kinds of Articles
Articles are of two types: indefinite and definite. A and An are indefinite articles while 'The' is called definite article.

Indefinite Articles (A, An)
The words 'a' and 'an' are indefinite articles. They are used before singular countable nouns.

'A' is used with the words that begin with a consonant sound.

Examples:
a book, a cat, a picture, a table, a lawyer

'A' is also used before the words (even if not a consonant) that begin with a 'u' sound. It is used before the word 'one' as well, although it begins with the vowel 'o' because it is pronounced 'wun'.

Examples:
a European country, a university, a uniform, a one-man army, a one-day seminar

'An' is used with words that begin with a vowel.

Examples:
an elephant, an owl, an apple, an item

'An' is also used before words that have a silent 'h' (not pronounced).

Examples:
an hour, an honest person

Definite Article (The)
The is a the definite article. It is used before a particular or definite persons or objects. It is used before all things that one-of-a-kind.

Examples:
the best doctor, the favourite student, the sweetest fruit

TRIVIA

A new word is added to the dictionary every two hours.

Uses of Articles

Uses of Indefinte articles – a, an

- **Before singular count nouns**

an is used before singular count nouns beginning with a vowel (a, e, i, o, u) or vowel sound:

Examples:

an apple, an elephant, an issue, an orange; a is used before singular count nouns beginning with consonants (other than a, e, i, o, u):

a stamp, a desk, a TV, a cup, a book

- **Before singular nouns that are unspecified:**
  a pencil, an orange

- **Before number collectives and some numbers:**
  a dozen, a gallon

- **Before a singular noun followed by a restrictive modifier:**
  A girl who was wearing a yellow hat.

- **With nouns to form adverbial phrases of quantity, amount, or degree:**

I felt a bit depressed.

Use of Definite Article (The)

- **To indicate a noun that is definite or has been previously specified in the context:**
  Please close the door.
  I like the clothes you gave me.
- **To indicate a noun that is unique:**
  Praise the Lord!
  The Columbia River is nearby.
- **To designate a natural phenomenon:**
  The nights get shorter in the summer.
  The wind is blowing so hard.
- **To refer to a time period:**
  I was very naïve in the past.
  This song was very popular in the 1980s.
- **To indicate all the members of a family:**
  I invited the Bakers for dinner.
  This medicine was invented by the Smiths.

Omission of Article

Some words do not require an article at all. Articles are omitted in these cases:

(a) **Before proper nouns.**
   Examples:
   India, Sri Lanka, Mahatma Gandhi
   The India is a developing country. (incorrect)
   India is a developing country. (correct)

(b) **Before common nouns when referring to the whole class in general.**
   Examples:
   Which flower is this?
   Are these golden rings?

(c) **Before abstract nouns when used in a general sense.**
   Examples:
   Necessity is the mother of invention.
   Charity begins at home.

- The words 'a' and 'an' are indefinite articles. They are used before singular countable nouns.
- The word 'the' is the definite article. It is used before a particular or definite persons or objects.

PRACTICE EXERCISE

I. **Fill in the blanks with correct article(s) given in the options.**

1. _____ Earth revolves around _____ Sun.
    (a) The, the (b) A, a
    (c) An, an (d) None

2. It feels good to perform in front of _____ appreciative audience.
    (a) The (b) A
    (c) An (d) None

3. My eyes hurt. I have to visit _____ eye-doctor.
    (a) The (b) A
    (c) An (d) None

4. Suddenly I heard the whirring sound of _____ helicopter.
    (a) The (b) A
    (c) An (d) None

5. _____ milk comes from cows.
    (a) The (b) A
    (c) An (d) None

6. My father was _____ honest man.
    (a) The (b) A
    (c) An (d) None

7. Tomorrow evening the whole world will be watching _____ Oscars.
    (a) The (b) A
    (c) An (d) None

8. _____ nightingale is _____ unique bird.
    (a) The, a (b) A, the
    (c) An, a (d) None

9. My favourite subject is _____ Philosophy.
    (a) The (b) A
    (c) An (d) None

10. _____ Dachshund is _____ national dog of Germany.
    (a) The, the
    (b) A, a
    (c) An, an
    (d) None

11. _____ sweeter _____ coffee, _____ better it tastes.
    (a) The, the, the (b) A, the, the
    (c) An, a, the (d) None

12. _____ water, when heated becomes _____ steam.
    (a) The, the (b) The, none
    (c) An, the (d) None

13. My grandparents lived in _____ one-room apartment.
    (a) The (b) A
    (c) An (d) None

14. _____ price of petrol keeps rising.
    (a) The (b) A
    (c) An (d) None

15. I would like _____ piece of cake.
    (a) The (b) A
    (c) An (d) None

16. Look at _____ woman over there. She is a famous actress.
    (a) The (b) A
    (c) An (d) None

17. _____ computers are useful machines.
    (a) The (b) A
    (c) An (d) None

18. Ben has _____ terrible headache.
    (a) The (b) A
    (c) An (d) None

19. _____ sugar is bad for your teeth.
    (a) The (b) A
    (c) An (d) None

20. Where is _____ book I lent you last week?
    (a) The (b) A
    (c) An (d) None

II. **Choose the correct sentence from the given options.**

1. (a) India is a democratic country.
   (b) The India is a democratic country.
   (c) India is the democratic country.
   (d) India is democratic country.

2. (a) That is a girl I told you about.
   (b) That is girl I told you about.
   (c) That is the girl I told you about.
   (d) That is an girl I told you about.

3. (a) We reached a hour ago.
   (b) We reached an hour ago.
   (c) We reached the hour ago.
   (d) We reached hour ago.

Articles 25

4. (a) Juan is Spanish.
   (b) Juan is the Spanish.
   (c) Juan is a Spanish.
   (d) Juan is an Spanish.
5. (a) I bought the new TV set yesterday.
   (b) I bought an new TV set yesterday.
   (c) I bought a new TV set yesterday.
   (d) I bought new TV set yesterday.
6. (a) He is engineer.
   (b) He is a engineer.
   (c) He is an engineer.
   (d) He is the engineer.
7. (a) I love reading the history books.
   (b) I love reading a history books.
   (c) I love reading an history books.
   (d) I love reading history books.
8. (a) I watched the video you had sent me.
   (b) I watched video you had sent me.
   (c) I watched a video you had sent me.
   (d) I watched an video you had sent me.
9. (a) I want to be a pilot when I grow up.
   (b) I want to be pilot when I grow up.
   (c) I want to be the pilot when I grow up.
   (d) I want to be an pilot when I grow up.
10. (a) A aeroplane flew over our heads a while back.
    (b) An aeroplane flew over our heads a while back.
    (c) Aeroplane flew over our heads a while back.
    (d) The aeroplane flew over our heads a while back.

HOTS

Fill in the blanks with appropriate article.

1. An atheist does not believe in _____ God.
   (a) a   (b) an
   (c) the   (d) none of these
2. He never listens to _____ classical music.
   (a) a   (b) an
   (c) the   (d) none of these
3. You can pay that bill at _____ bank.
   (a) a   (b) an
   (c) the   (d) none of these
4. My flat is on _____ second floor.
   (a) a   (b) an
   (c) the   (d) none of these
5. It was _____ excellent meal last night.
   (a) a   (b) an
   (c) the   (d) none of these
6. _____ Mercury is _____ liquid metal.
   (a) The, a   (b) The, the
   (c) No article, a (d) No article, the
7. _____ Chennai Express is _____ fastest train of all.
   (a) The, a   (b) The, the
   (c) No article, a (d) No article, the
8. _____ Prime Minister unfurled _____ national flag at _____ Red Fort.
   (a) A, a, the (b) An, an, a
   (c) The, the, the (d) No articles
9. He is _____ engineer but he wanted to be _____ dynamic economist.
   (a) a, the   (b) an, an
   (c) an, a   (d) No articles
10. Alexander Pope said that _____ honest man is _____ noblest work of God.
    (a) the, the   (b) an, a
    (c) an, an   (d) an, the

Verbs

Learning Objectives : In this chapter, students will learn about:
- ✓ Kinds of Verbs
- ✓ Modal verbs and their use
- ✓ Subject Verb Agreement

CHAPTER SUMMARY

Verbs are the words that show an action or a state of being.

Examples:
drive, eat, sing, fall, give, read, bounce

Kinds of Verbs

Verbs can be divided into three groups based on their use in a sentence.

Action Verbs

Action verbs express an action, e.g. give, drink, walk. These verbs can be either transitive or intransitive. A <u>transitive verb</u> always has a noun that follows the action of the verb, called the direct object. An <u>intransitive verb</u> does not need an object to make the sense complete.

Example:
Laura **raises** her hand

('Raises' is the verb and 'hand' is the object, which is required to make the complete sense of the sentence.) Thus, *'Raises'* is the transitive verb in this sentence.

He **swam** fast.

('Swam' is the verb. The word 'fast' modifies the verb, but there is no object required to make the sense complete.) Thus, *'swam'* is an intransitive verb.

Verbs of Being

Verbs of being express a state of existence. The most common of them are: 'am', 'are', 'is', 'was', and 'were'. They change form to agree with the subject.

Examples:
Lily **is** a student.

Penny **was** away last week.

Thus, the verbs – is, was – are showing the existence of the subject.

Auxiliary Verbs
Helping verbs

Auxiliary verbs are also called helping verbs. Helping verbs are used before main verbs to show the time of the action.

Example:
Jasmine **will** drive to work tomorrow. (In this sentence *'will'* is the helping verb and *'drive'* is the main verb.)

Tejas **is going** to Australia. (In this sentence *'is'* is the helping verb and *'going'* is the main verb.)

Modal verbs

Modal verbs are used with other verbs to show ability, obligation, permission, possibility etc. Modals are never used with other modal verbs.

Some modal verbs and their uses:

Shall (intent), *would* (polite requests), *should/must* (obligation or necessity), *can* (possibility), *could* (ability) and *may* (permission).

Examples:
How long **will** this work take to complete?

(In this sentence 'will' is used to state what we expect to happen. Thus, it is a modal verb.)

I **will** be finishing these exercises by the time you return home.

Will also expresses future activity.

Some auxiliary verbs:
am, is, are, was, were, may, might, must, has, have, had, should, does, do, did, will, would, shall, can, could

Subject-Verb Agreement

Basic Rule: A singular subject (John, she, car) takes a singular verb (is, goes, shines), whereas a plural subject takes a plural verb.

Examples:

The list of items is/are on the desk.

(If you know that list is the singular subject, then you will choose *is* for the verb).

Ruul 1: The subject comes before a phrase beginning with of. This is a key rule for understanding subjects.

Examples:

A bouquet of yellow roses lend colour and fragrance to the room. (Incorrect)

A bouquet of yellow roses lends colour and fragrance to the room (Correct)

(bouquet lends, not roses lend)

Rule 2: The singular subjects connected by or, either/or, or neither/nor require a singular verb.

Examples:

My aunt or my uncle is arriving by train today.

Neither Juan nor Carmen is available.

Either Kiana or Casey is helping with stage decorations today.

TRIVIA

English is the official language of Sky, all pilots, regardless of their country of origin, identify themselves in English on international flights.

Rule 3: The verb in sentences with or, either/or, neither/nor agrees with the noun or pronoun closest to it.

Examples:

Neither the plates nor the serving bowl goes on that shelf.

Neither the serving bowl nor the plates go on that shelf.

This rule can create problem. For example, if I is one of two (or more) subjects, it could lead to this odd sentence:

Neither she, my friends, nor I am going to the festival. (Awkward)

If possible, it's best to reword such grammatically correct but awkward sentences.

Neither she, I, nor my friends are going to the festival. (Better)

OR

She, my friends, and I are not going to the festival. (Correct)

Rule 4: As a general rule, use a plural verb with two or more subjects when they are connected by 'and'

Examples:

A car and a bike are my means of transportation.

Exceptions: Breaking and entering is against the law.

The bed and breakfast was charming.

(In these sentences, breaking and entering and bed and breakfast are compound nouns.)

Rule 5: Sometimes, the subject is separated from the verb by the words such as along with, as well as, besides, not, etc. These words and phrases are not part of the subject. Ignore them and use a singular verb when the subject is singular.

Examples:

The politician, along with the newsmen, is expected shortly.

Excitement, as well as nervousness, is the cause of her shaking.

Rule 6: In sentences beginning with here or there, the true subject follows the verb.

Examples:

There are four hurdles to jump.

There is a high hurdle to jump.

Here are the keys.

Note: The word there's, a contraction of there is, leads to bad habits in informal sentences like 'There's a lot of people here today', because it's easier to say 'there's' than 'there are.' Take care never to use there's with a plural subject.

Rule 7: Use a singular verb with distances, periods of time, sums of money, etc., when considered as a unit.

Examples:

Three miles is too far to walk.

Five years is the maximum sentence for that offense.

Ten dollars is a high price to pay.

But

Ten dollars (dollar bills) were scattered on the floor.

Rule 8: With words that indicate portions, e.g. a lot, a majority, some; if the subject is singular, use a singular verb. If it is plural, use a plural verb.

Examples:

A lot of the pie has disappeared.

A lot of the pies have disappeared.

A third of the city is unemployed.

A third of the people are unemployed.

All of the pie is gone.

All of the pies are gone.

Some of the pie is missing.

Some of the pies are missing.

Rule 9: With collective nouns such as group, jury, family, audience, population, the verb might be singular or plural, depending on the sense/intent of author.

Examples:

All of my family has arrived or have arrived.

Most of the jury is here OR are here.

A third of the population was not in favour or were not in favour of the bill.

Rule 10: The word 'were' replaces 'was' in sentences that express a wish or are contrary to fact:

Examples:

If John were here, you'd be sorry.

Shouldn't John be followed by was, not were, given that John is singular? But John isn't actually here, so we say were, not was.

(The sentence demonstrates the subjunctive mood, which is used to express things that are hypothetical, wishful, imaginary, or factually contradictory. The subjunctive mood pairs singular subjects with what we usually think of as plural verbs.)

Examples:

I wish it were Friday.

She requested that he raise his hand.

In the first example, a wishful statement, not a fact, is being expressed; therefore, were, which we usually think of as a plural verb, is used with the singular subject I.

Normally, he raise would sound terrible to us. However, in the second example, where a request is being expressed, the subjunctive mood is correct.

MUST REMEMBER

- A <u>transitive verb</u> always has a noun that follows the action of the verb, called the direct object. An <u>intransitive verb</u> does not need an object to make the sense complete.
- Modal verbs are used with other verbs to show ability, obligation, permission, possibility etc.

PRACTICE EXERCISE

I. Choose the correct option and fill in blanks in the sentences given below.

1. The elephant _____ all over the plants.
   (a) walking (b) ate
   (c) trampled (d) sit
2. The pizza _____ slowly in the brick oven.
   (a) cooks (b) lay
   (c) catches (d) grew
3. The computer _____ with a loud beep.
   (a) slid (b) stop
   (c) makes (d) started
4. I am not _____ to stay out after midnight.
   (a) allow (b) like
   (c) afraid (d) go
5. It is time to _____ our meeting for the day.
   (a) started (b) called
   (c) add (d) end
6. We _____ the game as a result of our great teamwork.
   (a) won (b) lose
   (c) loose (d) win
7. The students _____ to class after recess.
   (a) left (b) hurry
   (c) take (d) study
8. Eugene _____ a drum from a big metal can.
   (a) bought (b) caught
   (c) made (d) thought
9. Sierra _____ to do her own thing and never to follow the herd.
   (a) likes (b) try
   (c) proud (d) makes
10. The loaf of bread began to _____.
    (a) rise (b) fallen
    (c) decayed (d) make

II. Choose the correct form of the verb (of being) that best completes each sentence.

1. We _____ seldom as perfect or as accurate as we would like to be.
   (a) is (b) are
   (c) was (d) am
2. I _____ hungry now.
   (a) is (b) are
   (c) was (d) am
3. A funeral _____ certainly not an opportune time to tell your favourite joke.
   (a) was (b) are
   (c) is (d) am
4. He _____ late yesterday.
   (a) is (b) are
   (c) was (d) am
5. The brown fur of sloths _____ sometimes covered in green algae.
   (a) is (b) are
   (c) was (d) am
6. The climate in the mountains _____ cold and dry.
   (a) am (b) are
   (c) is (d) was
7. There _____ numerous benefits of learning how to read
   (a) is (b) are
   (c) was (d) am
8. His plays _____ personal dramas, often presented in a historical context.
   (a) are (b) is
   (c) was (d) am
9. Last year, John and Simon _____ working.
   (a) is (b) were
   (c) was (d) am
10. I _____ asleep yesterday afternoon when you called.
    (a) is (b) was
    (c) are (d) am

III. Choose the correct option to mark the type of the underlined verb in the following sentences.

1. The storm <u>broke</u>.
   (a) Transitive (b) Intransitive
   (c) Helping (d) Modal
2. As soon as the wind <u>blows</u>, the fog will clear.
   (a) Transitive (b) Intransitive
   (c) Helping (d) Modal
3. There <u>are</u> lots of things to buy.
   (a) Transitive (b) Intransitive
   (c) Helping (d) Modal
4. I <u>understood</u> her question.
   (a) Transitive (b) Intransitive
   (c) Helping (d) Modal

5. You <u>may</u> leave the room.
   (a) Transitive (b) Intransitive
   (c) Helping (d) Modal
6. She <u>sang</u> loudly.
   (a) Transitive (b) Intransitive
   (c) Helping (d) Modal
7. I think I <u>can</u> get you a ticket to the concert.
   (a) Transitive (b) Intransitive
   (c) Helping (d) Modal
8. He <u>could</u> speak Japanese when he was young.
   (a) Transitive (b) Intransitive
   (c) Helping (d) Modal
9. The mother <u>praised</u> her son.
   (a) Transitive (b) Intransitive
   (c) Helping (d) Modal
10. We <u>drove</u> to San Francisco.
    (a) Transitive (b) Intransitive
    (c) Helping (d) Modal

IV. **Choose the correct option to fill in the blanks with suitable auxiliary verbs.**
1. You ___ go only if you have permission.
   (a) may (b) did
   (c) was (d) is
2. We ___ have done the work, if we had the time.
   (a) will (b) would
   (c) are (d) were
3. He ___ writing a novel.
   (a) are (b) could
   (c) shall (d) is
4. They ___ marching forward
   (a) are (b) may
   (c) might (d) shall
5. They ___ engaged in a heated argument.
   (a) should (b) were
   (c) was (d) would
6. I ___ forgotten to post the letter.
   (a) have (b) may
   (c) can (d) has
7. They ___ violated the agreement.
   (a) has (b) could
   (c) have (d) should
8. I ___ explain the point to you.
   (a) does (b) can
   (c) were (d) was
9. I ___ going on a holiday.
   (a) am (b) could
   (c) would (d) should
10. The robbers stole whatever they ___ find in the shop.
    (a) can (b) could
    (c) should (d) would

HOTS

I. **Fill in the blanks with correct form of verb.**
1. Usually, I _____ parties but I _____ this very much.
   (a) enjoy / am not enjoying
   (b) am enjoying / haven't enjoyed
   (c) enjoy / don't enjoy
   (d) enjoyed / haven't enjoyed
2. It _____ quite often in Britain during the winter.
   (a) is snowing (b) snows
   (c) has been snowing (d) has snowed
3. Normally, I _____ to bed at around 11.30 every night.
   (a) am going
   (b) have been going
   (c) go
   (d) have gone
4. There is something wrong with her car at the moment so she _____ to work by bus this week.
   (a) has been going
   (b) goes
   (c) went
   (d) is going
5. The River Ganges _____ through plains.
   (a) is flowing
   (b) has been flowing
   (c) flows
   (d) has flowed

II.

1. In which of the following sentences the verbs used are transitive?
   A : Zack eats.
   B : Ronaldo plays football.
   C : Lata sings a song.
   (a) Only A
   (b) A and B
   (c) Only C
   (d) B and C

2. Identify the type of verb in the following sentences.
   Hanna is beautiful.
   (a) Transitive verb
   (b) Intransitive verb
   (c) Linking verb
   (d) Auxiliary

3. Identify the type of verb in the following sentences.
   Jack writes a letter.
   (a) Transitive verb
   (b) Intransitive verb
   (c) Linking verb
   (d) Auxiliary

4. Identify the second form of verbs given in CAPITAL letters.
   QUIT
   (a) Quit
   (b) Quitted
   (c) Quits
   (d) Quitting

5. Identify the second form of verbs given in CAPITAL letters.
   SHINE
   (a) Shone
   (b) Shine
   (c) Shines
   (d) Shoned

Adverbs 6

Learning Objectives: In this chapter, students will learn about:
- Basics of Adverbs
- Types of Adverbs
- Uses of Adverbs

CHAPTER SUMMARY

Adverbs are the words that describe a verb, an adjective or another adverb. Adverbs answer the questions – when, where, how, why and how much or in what degree.

Examples:
Rohan runs fast. (Here, the word 'fast' adds to the meaning of verb 'runs'),
Thus, adverbs add to the meaning of a verb, another adverb, an adjective.

Types of Adverbs
Adverbs serve many functions and are divided according to their role in a sentence.

Adverb of place
These adverbs describe the place of an action.
Example:
The dog follows its master **everywhere**. (Adverb of place: everywhere)

Adverb of manner
These adverbs show the manner of doing an action.
Example:
The child is sleeping **soundly**. (Adverb of manner: soundly)

Adverb of time
These adverbs show the time of an action.
Example:
What are you going to do **tonight**? (Adverb of time: tonight)

Adverb of reason/result
These adverbs express the reason of an action.

Example:
I was ill, **therefore** I missed school. (Adverb of reason: therefore)

Adverb of degree
These adverbs show the degree of an action or an another adverb.
Example:
This team plays **very** well. (Adverb of degree: very)

Formation of Adverbs
Adverbs can be formed by adding 'ly' to nouns, verbs and adjectives.

Sleep (verb)	Sleepily (adverb)
Clever (adjective)	Cleverly (adverb)
Day (noun)	Daily (adverb)
Noise (noun)	Noisily (adverb)

Adverbs that do not end with 'ly' are called **irregular adverbs**.
Examples:
soon, often, yet, so, rather, around, never.

Uses of Adverbs
- Many adverbs end in -ly, but many do not. Generally, if a word can have -ly added to its adjective form, place it there to form an adverb.
  Examples:
  She thinks quick/quickly.

How does she think? Quickly.
(She is a quick/quickly thinker. Quick is an adjective describing thinker, so no -ly is attached)

She thinks fast/fastly.
(Fast answers the question how, so it is an adverb. But fast never has -ly attached to it.)

We performed bad/badly.
(Badly describes how we performed, so -ly is added)

- Don't add -ly with linking verbs such as taste, smell, look, feel, which pertain to the senses. Adverbs are often misplaced in such sentences, which require adjectives instead.

Examples:
Roses smell sweet/sweetly.
(In this case, smell is a linking verb – which requires an adjective to modify roses – so no -ly.)

The woman looked angry/angrily to us. (Adjective)
(We are describing her appearance (she appeared angry), so no -ly is added.)

The woman looked angry/angrily at the paint splotches. (Adverb-Angrily)
(Here, the woman actively looked (used her eyes), so the -ly is added.)

She feels bad/badly about the news.
(She is not feeling with fingers, so no -ly is added.)

- The word good is an adjective, whose adverb equivalent is well.

Examples:
You did a good job.
(Good describes the job.)
You did the job well.
(Well answers how.)
You smell good today.
(Good describes your fragrance, not how you smell with your nose, so using the adjective is correct.)
You smell well for someone with a cold.
(You are actively smelling with your nose here, so use the adverb.)

- The word *well* can be an adjective too. While referring to health, we often use *well* rather than *good*.

Examples:
You do not look well today.
I don't feel well, either.

TRIVIA

"Typewriter" is one of the longest common words you can type on the top row of a typewriter.

- Adjectives come in three forms, also called degrees. An adjective in its normal or usual form is called an adjective of positive degree. There are also comparative and superlative degrees, which are used for comparison as follows:

Examples:

Positive	Comparative	Superlative
sweet	sweeter	sweetest
bad	worse	worst
efficient	more efficient	most efficient

A common error in using adjectives and adverbs arises from using the wrong form of comparison. To compare two things, always use a comparative adjective:

Example:
She is the cleverer of the two women (never cleverest)
(The word cleverest is the superlative form of clever. Use it only when comparing three or more things.)

Examples:
She is the cleverest of them all.
Chocolate or vanilla: which do you like best? **(Incorrect)**
Chocolate or vanilla: which do you like better? **(Correct)**

- There are also three degrees of adverbs. In formal usage, do not drop the -ly from an adverb while using the comparative form.

Examples:
She spoke quicker than he did. **(Incorrect)**
She spoke more quickly than he did. **(Correct)**
Talk quieter. **(Incorrect)**
Talk more quietly. **(Correct)**

Key Points

- Adverbs answer the question how (e.g. How is the dog running?), as well as when, and where.

  Example:
  The dog ran quickly.
  (*Quickly* is modifying the verb *ran*.)

- The adverb doesn't have to go after the verb.

  Example:
  Silently, the girl snuck past her parents' room.

- Adverbs can also modify adjectives and other adverbs.

  Example:
  The dog ran fairly quickly.
  (The adverb *fairly* is modifying the other adverb *quickly*.)

  Example:
  The weather report is almost always right.
  (The adverb *almost* is modifying the adverb *always*.)

  Example:
  The woman is quite pretty.
  (The adverb *quite* is modifying the adjective *pretty*.)

  Example:
  This book is more interesting than the last one.
  (The adverb *more* is modifying the adjective *interesting*.)

MUST REMEMBER

→ Adverbs are the words that describe a verb, an adjective or another adverb.
→ Adverbs that do not end with 'ly' are called **irregular adverbs**.
→ Don't add -ly with linking verbs such as taste, smell, look, feel, which pertain to the senses. Adverbs are often misplaced in such sentences, which require adjectives instead.
→ An adjective in its normal or usual form is called an adjective of positive degree.

PRACTICE EXERCISE

I. Choose the correct options which the underlined adverbs describe.

1. Thank you for answering my call so <u>quickly</u>.
   (a) call (b) answering
   (c) you (d) my

2. Alisha <u>frantically</u> searched for her note-book after working on it many hours the previous night.
   (a) notebook (b) searched
   (c) working (d) hours

3. Justin wandered <u>aimlessly</u> through the forest in search of his campsite.
   (a) through (b) campsite
   (c) forest (d) wandered

4. After our meal every night, we stroll <u>leisurely</u> in the nearby park.
   (a) meal (b) park
   (c) stroll (d) night

5. She sang so <u>heartily</u> that the baby fell asleep.
   (a) sang (b) baby
   (c) she (d) asleep

6. He pushed the door <u>forcefully</u>.
   (a) door (b) he
   (c) pushed (d) the

7. I <u>vaguely</u> remember my childhood days.
   (a) remember (b) days
   (c) childhood (d) my

8. Andrew <u>recently</u> began collecting stamps from various countries.
   (a) collecting (b) began
   (c) stamps (d) countries

9. Caleb woke up <u>suddenly</u> when he heard the sound of thunder.
   (a) heard (b) woke
   (c) sound (d) thunder

10. He laughed <u>heartily</u> when he heard the funny story.
    (a) heard (b) story
    (c) funny (d) laughed

II. Choose the correct adverbs to fill in the blanks.

1. Natalie was sad because she scored _____ on her math test.
   (a) badly (b) extremely
   (c) nicely (d) strongly

2. As soon as you are ready, we will _____ leave for the concert.
   (a) obviously (b) promptly
   (c) cleverly (d) usefully

3. Coming up with new concepts is not easy. Only people who can think _____ can participate in this contest.
   (a) foolishly (b) lastly
   (c) hurriedly (d) creatively

4. Even after several warnings, Sarah failed to reach on time _____.
   (a) continually (b) annually
   (c) usefully (d) carefully

5. We will _____ give up.
   (a) never (b) since
   (c) much (d) very

6. Brenda was sad to go, but she promised to visit _____ again.
   (a) never (b) soon
   (c) only (d) always

7. _____ aim high.
   (a) early (b) easily
   (c) always (d) never

8. The maid dropped the vase _____.
   (a) sweetly (b) carefully
   (c) happily (d) accidentally

9. Olivia's mom _____ walks to school with her.
   (a) angrily (b) usually
   (c) too (d) softly

10. These boys work _____ harder than those.
    (a) much (b) very
    (c) rarely (d) never

11. My parents _____ punished me when they found out that I had cheated on my history test.
    (a) happily (b) proudly
    (c) never (d) immediately

12. He started _____ but then ran _____ to finish first.
    (a) slowly, quickly (b) fast, slow
    (c) quickly, slowly (d) slow, fast

III. **Choose the correct options to fill in the blanks in the following sentences.**
    (Hint: Form adverbs by adding "ly" to suitable words. The first one is done for you.)

1. It was <u>really</u> kind of you to help me.
   (a) real (correct option)
   (b) pure
   (c) horrible
   (d) faithful

2. She was sleeping so _____ that she did not want to wake up.
   (a) hurry   (b) harm
   (c) comfortable (d) frighten

3. This experiment can go _____ wrong.
   (a) terrible   (b) act
   (c) clever   (d) lucky

4. Jason _____ finished all the cookies without saving any for his brother.
   (a) aimless   (b) selfish
   (c) noise   (d) sad

5. I need help. _____ you are here.
   (a) Thankful   (b) Beautiful
   (c) Useful   (d) Truthful

6. Meet Roy and Sue. They are a _____ married couple.
   (a) rare   (b) happy
   (c) kind   (d) accident

7. Robert's eyes opened _____ when he saw the snake.
   (a) sleep   (b) last
   (c) dim   (d) wide

8. I have not finished my work _____. Some of it is left.
   (a) complete   (b) part
   (c) full   (d) total

9. Mother loves me and my sister _____.
   (a) equal   (b) harm
   (c) sad   (d) hurry

HOTS

I. **Fill in the blanks with appropriate adverb.**

1. They called the police _____ after the accident.
   (a) immediately (b) slowly
   (c) peacefully   (d) none of these

2. Kiran is a _____ paid employee of this company.
   (a) lowly   (b) highly
   (c) hardly   (d) none of these

3. I was stuck in a jam for _____ two hours.
   (a) nearly   (b) simply
   (c) correctly   (d) none of these

4. How _____ do you go there?
   (a) never   (b) seldom
   (c) often   (d) none of these

5. Raman was _____ happy when he got his first job.
   (a) extremely   (b) fully
   (c) halfly   (d) none of these

II. **Identify the adverbs of manner, place, time or frequency underlined in the given sentences:**

1. Have you met him <u>before</u>?
   (a) Manner   (b) Place
   (c) Time   (d) Frequency

2. He was sleeping <u>upstairs</u>.
   (a) Manner   (b) Place
   (c) Time   (d) Frequency

3. Do you <u>often</u> play cricket.
   (a) Manner   (b) Place
   (c) Time   (d) Frequency

4. Please, listen to me <u>attentively</u>.
   (a) Manner   (b) Place
   (c) Time   (d) Frequency

5. I came to know about your friend <u>afterwards</u>.
   (a) Manner   (b) Place
   (c) Time   (d) Frequency

Prepositions   7

Learning Objectives : In this chapter, students will learn about:
- ✓ Basics of Preposition
- ✓ Kinds of Preposition
- ✓ Uses of Preposition

CHAPTER SUMMARY

Prepositions are the words that show a relationship between two nouns or between a noun or a pronoun and the remaining words in a sentence.

Examples:
He waited for me **at** the crossing.
We are **against** child labour.
The cat went and hid **under** the table.
Some commonly used prepositions are:

About	Beyond	Since	Above
By	Through	Across	Down
Till	After	During	To
Against	Except	Towards	Along
For	Under	Amid	From
Until	Among	In	Up
Around	Into	Upon	At
Near	With	Before	Of
Within	Behind	Off	Without
Below	On	Beside	Over
Between			

Kinds of Preposition
Prepositions are of five kinds:

Simple Prepositions
Simple prepositions are words like in, on, at, about, over, under, off, of, for, to etc.

Examples:
She sat **on** the sofa.
There is some water **in** the bottle.
They sat **around** the table.

Compound Prepositions
Compound prepositions are usually formed from two simple prepositions. Some compound prepositions are: without, within, inside, outside, into, beneath, below, behind, between etc.

Examples:
He fell into the river.
She sat between her kids.

Double Prepositions
Double prepositions are words like outside of, out of, from behind, from beneath etc.

Examples:
Suddenly, he emerged <u>from behind</u> the curtain.
He walked <u>out of</u> the compound.

Participle Prepositions
Participle prepositions are words like concerning, notwithstanding, pending, considering etc.

Examples:
There was little chance of success, <u>notwithstanding</u> they decided to go ahead.
You did the job well, <u>considering</u> your age and inexperience.

Phrase Prepositions
Phrase prepositions are phrases like because of, by means of, with regard to, on behalf of, instead of, on account of, in opposition to, for the sake of etc.

Examples:

The match was cancelled <u>because of</u> the rain.

He succeeded <u>by means of</u> perseverance.

Uses of ON
On is used to:

- **Express a surface of something**

  Examples:

  I put an egg <u>on</u> the kitchen table.

  The paper is <u>on</u> my desk.

- **Specify days and dates**

  Examples:

  The garbage truck comes <u>on</u> Wednesdays.

  I was born <u>on</u> the 14th day of June in 1988.

- **Indicate a device or machine, such as a phone or computer**

  Examples:

  He is <u>on</u> the phone right now.

  She has been <u>on</u> the computer since this morning.

  My favorite movie will be <u>on</u> TV tonight.

- **Indicate a part of the body**

  Examples:

  The stick hit me <u>on</u> my shoulder.

  He kissed me <u>on</u> my cheek.

  I wear a ring <u>on</u> my finger.

- **Indicate the state of something**

  Examples:

  Everything in this store is <u>on</u> sale.

  The building is <u>on</u> fire.

> **TRIVIA**
>
> A 672-sided shape is called a "hexahectaheptacontakaidigon"

Uses of AT
At is used to:

- **Point out specific time**

  Examples:

  I will meet you <u>at</u> 12 p.m.

  The bus will stop here <u>at</u> 5:45 p.m.

- **Indicate a place**

  Examples:

  There is a party <u>at</u> the club house.

  There were hundreds of people <u>at</u> the park.

  We saw a baseball game <u>at</u> the stadium.

- **Indicate an email address**

  Examples:

  Please email me <u>at</u> abc@defg.com.

- **Indicate an activity**

  Examples:

  He laughed <u>at</u> my acting.

  I am good <u>at</u> drawing a portrait.

Uses of IN
In is used to/for:

- **Unspecific times during a day, month, season, year**

  Examples:

  She always reads newspapers <u>in</u> the morning.

  <u>In</u> the summer, we have a rainy season for three weeks.

  The new semester will start <u>in</u> March.

- **Indicate a location or place**

  Examples:

  She looked me directly <u>in</u> the eyes.

  I am currently staying <u>in</u> a hotel.

  My hometown is Los Angeles, which is <u>in</u> California.

- **Indicate a shape, color, or size**

  Examples:

  This painting is mostly <u>in</u> blue.

  The students stood <u>in</u> a circle.

  This jacket comes <u>in</u> four different sizes.

- **Express while doing something**

  Examples:

  In preparing <u>for</u> the final report, we revised the tone three times.

  A catch phrase needs to be impressive in marketing a product.

- **Indicate a belief, opinion, interest, or feeling**

  Examples:

  I believe <u>in</u> the next life.

  We are not interested <u>in</u> gambling.

Uses of OF
Of is used to/for:

- **Belonging to, relating to, or connected with**
  Examples:
  The secret of this game is that you can't ever win.
  The highlight of the show is at the end.
  I always dreamed of being rich and famous.

- **Indicate reference**
  Examples:
  I got married in the summer of 2000.
  This is a picture of my family.
  I got a discount of 10 percent on the purchase.

- **Indicate an amount or number**
  Examples:
  I drank three cups of milk.
  A large number of people gathered to protest.
  I had only four hours of sleep during the last two days.

Uses of TO
To is used to:

- **Indicate the place, person, or thing that someone or something moves toward, or the direction of something.**
  Examples:
  I am heading to the entrance of the building.
  All of us went to the movie theater.
  Please send it back to me.

- **Indicate a limit or an ending point**
  Examples:
  The snow was piled up to the roof.
  The stock prices rose up to 100 dollars.

- **Indicate a relationship:**
  Examples:
  This letter is very important to your admission.
  Do not respond to every little thing in your life.

- **Indicate a time or a period**
  Examples:
  I work nine to six, Monday to Friday.
  It is now 10 to five.

Uses of FOR
For is used to/for:

- **Indicate the use of something**
  Examples:
  I baked a cake for your birthday.
  I put a note on the door for privacy.
  She has been studying hard for the final exam.

- **Mean because of**
  Examples:
  I am so happy for you.
  We feel deeply sorry for your loss.

- **Indicate time or duration**
  Examples:
  He's been famous for many decades.
  I attended the university for one year only.

MUST REMEMBER

- Prepositions are the words that show a relationship between two nouns or between a noun or a pronoun and the remaining words in a sentence.
- Compound prepositions are usually formed from two simple prepositions.

PRACTICE EXERCISE

I. Choose the correct options to fill in the blanks with prepositions.

1. He has changed _____ the punishment he received.
   (a) so (b) to
   (c) from (d) after

2. The shop remains closed _____ Sundays.
   (a) on (b) of
   (c) in (d) from

3. My father is _____ my returning home late.
   (a) between (b) against
   (c) before (d) after

4. He waited for me _____ the station.
   (a) at (b) about
   (c) down (d) during

5. There is no point beating _____ the bush.
   (a) on (b) above
   (c) under (d) around

6. You should put your family _____ everything else.
   (a) under (b) before
   (c) after (d) in

7. I am running _____ schedule.
   (a) behind (b) beside
   (c) to (d) in

8. I was _____ the flat when the incident took place.
   (a) under (b) over
   (c) toward (d) below

9. There is no public holiday _____ May and August.
   (a) in (b) between
   (c) from (d) to

10. He passed _____ the park on his way home.
    (a) up (b) till
    (c) by (d) near

11. Run _____ quickly and get me some eggs.
    (a) down (b) over
    (c) in (d) on

12. It is not good to borrow money _____ anyone.
    (a) off (b) for
    (c) upon (d) from

13. There are a lot of clothes stuffed _____ the cupboard.
    (a) on (b) inside
    (c) outside (d) over

14. I wanted to talk to you _____ yesterday's quarrel.
    (a) upon (b) around
    (c) about (d) amid

15. The teacher asked the students to put _____ their pens.
    (a) on (b) down
    (c) in (d) out

16. I am responsible _____ training the new recruits.
    (a) at (b) about
    (c) with (d) for

17. I was not quite satisfied _____ the exam results.
    (a) at (b) for
    (c) with (d) about

18. Our atmosphere consists _____ oxygen, nitrogen and carbon dioxide.
    (a) into (b) of
    (c) with (d) for

19. Diwali is celebrated _____ India in October.
    (a) through
    (b) from
    (c) towards (d) across

20. He got married _____ the age of 28.
    (a) at (b) in
    (c) on (d) for

II. Choose the correct option/sentence in each set given below.

1. (a) I didn't have enough money to pay for the meal.
   (b) I didn't have enough money on pay for the meal.
   (c) I didn't have enough money for pay for the meal.
   (d) I didn't have enough money at pay for the meal.

Prepositions

2. (a) Jane goes to the office early in Tuesdays.
   (b) Jane goes to the office early for Tuesdays.
   (c) Jane goes to the office early on Tuesdays.
   (d) Jane goes to the office early upon Tuesdays.
3. (a) Ten people were killed when a bus collided at a car.
   (b) Ten people were killed when a bus collided on a car.
   (c) Ten people were killed when a bus collided towards a car.
   (d) Ten people were killed when a bus collided with a car.
4. (a) I'm dreaming into becoming a famous scientist one day.
   (b) I'm dreaming about becoming a famous scientist one day.
   (c) I'm dreaming for becoming a famous scientist one day.
   (d) I'm dreaming with becoming a famous scientist one day.
5. (a) My cousin is married to a famous actor.
   (b) My cousin is married with a famous actor.
   (c) My cousin is married for a famous actor.
   (d) My cousin is married from a famous actor.
6. (a) She insisted with helping me with the dishes.
   (b) She insisted for helping me with the dishes.
   (c) She insisted about helping me with the dishes.
   (d) She insisted on helping me with the dishes.
7. (a) I bought many things in my stay in New York.
   (b) I bought many things during my stay in New York.
   (c) I bought many things on my stay in New York.
   (d) I bought many things within my stay in New York.
8. (a) We entered the building at the back entrance.
   (b) We entered the building by the back entrance.
   (c) We entered the building through the back entrance.
   (d) We entered the building to the back entrance.
9. (a) I am very fond at drinking green tea.
   (b) I am very fond for drinking green tea.
   (c) I am very fond of drinking green tea.
   (d) I am very fond about drinking green tea.
10. (a) At the moment, she is recovering from her injuries.
    (b) At the moment, she is recovering at her injuries.
    (c) At the moment, she is recovering of her injuries.
    (d) At the moment, she is recovering with her injuries.

HOTS

I. **Fill in the blanks with the appropriate preposition.**

1. He congratulated you _____ your promotion.
   (a) in   (b) on
   (c) of   (d) for
2. She jumped _____ the river.
   (a) on   (b) in
   (c) into   (d) to
3. The jug is filled _____ milk.
   (a) of   (b) with
   (c) in   (d) upon
4. My wife is good _____ French.
   (a) in   (b) on
   (c) with   (d) at
5. I am fond _____ reading novel.
   (a) of   (b) by
   (c) on   (d) with

II. **Fill in the blanks with correct prepositions.**

1. I had _____ travel _____ a crowded train.
   (a) to, in   (b) at, at
   (c) at, by   (d) upon, in

2. He came back _____ India _____ 1972.
   (a) in, at   (b) on, to
   (c) to, in   (d) at, on
3. She lived _____ his opinion _____ 1970 _____ 1980.
   (a) in, from, to (b) at, on, to
   (c) in, to, a   (d) to, from, at
4. There was a big clock _____ the painting.
   (a) at   (b) beneath
   (c) below   (d) besides
5. When I reached the river, I simply swam _____.
   (a) beneath   (b) across
   (c) below   (d) in

Conjunctions 8

Learning Objectives : In this chapter, students will learn about:
- ✓ Concept of Coordinating Conjunction
- ✓ Basics of Subordinating Conjunction
- ✓ Correlative Conjunctions

CHAPTER SUMMARY

Conjunctions are linking words. They join words, phrases and sentences together. They play a very important role in the construction of sentences.

Coordinating Conjunction

Coordinating conjunctions join two thoughts (words or phrases) that are equally important in a sentence. The two thoughts they join are complete and can exist on their own as well.

Some coordinating conjunctions: For, And, Nor, But, Or, Yet, So

- **For** explains reason or purpose.

   Example:
   I go to the park every Sunday, *for* I like to take long walks.

- **And** adds one thing to another.

   Example:
   I like to go to the park every Sunday *and* take a long walk.

- **Nor** presents an alternative.

   Example:
   I don't like to go to the park *nor* do I like walking.

- **But** establishes contrast.

   Example:
   I like to go to the park *but* I hate walking.

- **Or** gives a choice.

   Example:
   I stay at home on Sunday evenings *or* I go to the park.

- **Yet** contrasts one idea with another, which follow each other logically.

   Example:
   I always take a book to the park, *yet* I never read.

- **So** shows effect or consequence.

   Example:
   I have bought new running shoes, *so* I have to go to the park.

TRIVIA

The word "selfie" was the Oxford Dictionary's Word of the Year in 2013 because the use of the term increased 17,000% from 2012 to 2013.

Subordinating Conjunction

Subordinating conjunctions are used to join two thoughts (words or phrases) where one of the thoughts is dependent on the other for meaning or relevance. The dependent thought cannot exist on its own in a sentence.

Examples:

Since the boys misbehaved, they were punished.

She left early because her parents called.

Wait here until I return.

Before the school reopens, we must finish our holiday homework.

Once you are home, have a chat with your sister.

As soon as the cake is baked, we shall have it.

Commonly used subordinating conjunctions include:

After, although, as, as soon as, because, before, by the time, even if, even though, if, in case, rather than, since, so that, though, until, when, whenever, where, whereas, wherever, whether, while, how

Correlative Conjunctions

Correlative conjunctions are a pair of conjunctions that are always used together.

Both/and

Examples:

She won gold medals from both single and group races.

Either/or

Examples:

I am fine with either Monday or Wednesday.

Neither/nor

Examples:

Neither you nor I will get off early today.

Not only/but also

Examples:

Not only red but also green looks good on you.

MUST REMEMBER

- Conjunctions are linking words. They join words, phrases and sentences together.
- Coordinating conjunctions join two thoughts that are equally important in a sentence.
- Subordinating conjunctions are used to join two thoughts where one of the thoughts is dependent on the other for meaning or relevance.
- Correlative conjunctions are a pair of conjunctions that are always used together.

PRACTICE EXERCISE

I. **Fill in the blanks with correct options (coordinating conjunction).**

1. I was rushing to my appointment, _____ I didn't make it on time.
   (a) and   (b) so
   (c) for   (d) yet

2. I got an A in my history test _____ I did well in Maths too.
   (a) and   (b) nor
   (c) yet   (d) so

3. I have just eaten dinner _____ I am not hungry.
   (a) and   (b) or
   (c) so   (d) but

4. You better hurry _____ you will be late for work.
   (a) and   (b) or
   (c) so   (d) but

5. He must be asleep _____ there is no light in his room.
   (a) but   (b) and
   (c) nor   (d) for

6. David knew he was wrong, _____ he apologized.
   (a) so   (b) for
   (c) and   (d) but

7. I waited for hours _____ she did not come.
   (a) but   (b) for
   (c) so   (d) and

8. I am bored. Let's go out for dinner _____ see a movie.
   (a) so   (b) yet
   (c) and   (d) but

9. Are you busy this weekend _____ do you have some free time?
   (a) and   (b) or
   (c) but   (d) for

10. Bela's just got a promotion at work _____ she is very happy.
    (a) and   (b) but
    (c) yet   (d) so

II. **Fill in the blanks with correct options (subordinating conjunction).**

1. _____ it's raining, I am staying in.
   (a) as   (b) when
   (c) so that   (d) in case

2. You will succeed _____ you work hard.
   (a) before   (b) until
   (c) if   (d) although

3. I don't know _____ she will come.
   (a) after   (b) whether
   (c) before   (d) though

4. _____ she is poor, she is honest.
   (a) Since
   (b) Because
   (c) Though
   (d) After

5. _____ I liked him, I tried to help.
   (a) Although (b) Because
   (c) That   (d) Until

6. I will bring my cat _____ you are allergic.
   (a) unless   (b) if
   (c) because   (d) since

7. We can travel _____ land or water.
   (a) before   (b) by
   (c) so that   (d) when

8. The train had left _____ we reached the station.
   (a) after   (b) since
   (c) before   (d) though

9. We haven't had a get-together _____ you left.
   (a) since
   (b) even though
   (c) although
   (d) though

10. Give me something to eat, _____ I will die of hunger.
    (a) unless   (b) else
    (c) until   (d) since

HOTS

Fill in the blanks with correct options (correlative conjunction).

1. _____ Mom _____ Dad will pick you up.
   (a) Either/or
   (b) Neither/nor
   (c) Both/and
   (d) Not only/but also

2. He is _____ intelligent _____ good-natured.
   (a) Either/or
   (b) Neither/nor
   (c) Both/and
   (d) Not only/but also

3. _____ the husband _____ the wife will be coming.
   (a) Either/or
   (b) Neither/nor
   (c) Both/and
   (d) Not only/but also

4. _____ the husband _____ the wife came.
   (a) Either/or
   (b) Neither/nor
   (c) Both/and
   (d) Not only/but also

5. _____ Alice, _____ John got the scholarship.
   (a) Either/or
   (b) Neither/nor
   (c) Both/and
   (d) Not only/but also

6. I _____ love _____ respect parents.
   (a) Either/or
   (b) Neither/nor
   (c) Both/and
   (d) Not only/but also

7. He _____ tells lies _____ misbehaves with everybody.
   (a) Either/or
   (b) Neither/nor
   (c) Both/and
   (d) Not only/but also

8. You must _____ obey me _____ quit.
   (a) Either/or
   (b) Neither/nor
   (c) Both/and
   (d) Not only/but also

9. _____ Alex _____ Carlos applied for the job.
   (a) Either/or
   (b) Neither/nor
   (c) Both/and
   (d) Not only/but also

10. The shop has _____ tea _____ coffee.
    (a) Either/or
    (b) Neither/nor
    (c) Both/and
    (d) Not only/but also

Conjunctions

Phrasal Verbs

Learning Objectives : In this chapter, students will learn about:
- Basics of Phrasal verbs
- Types of Phrasal verbs

CHAPTER SUMMARY

Phrasal verbs are formed when a verb is followed by another word which is known as a participle. The participle may be an adverb or a preposition. The verb and the participle together form completely different meaning from the verb alone.

The usage of phrasal verbs in writing and speech is considered good.

The following are some phrasal verbs with their meanings.

Phrasal Verb	Meaning
Ask around	Ask many people the same thing
Add up to something	Equal
Blow up	Explode
Break down	Stop functioning
Break in	Enter forcefully
Break up	End a relationship
Call off	Cancel
Catch up	To get to the same point as someone else
Cheer up	Become happier
Chip in	Help/contribute
Come across	Find unexpectedly
Count on	Rely
Do away with	Discard
Dress up	Wear nice clothes
Drop out	Quit a class/Project
Eat out	Eat in a restaurant
Fall apart	Break into pieces
Figure out	Understand

Find out	Discover
Get along	Like each other
Get back	Return
Give up	Stop trying
Go ahead	Start
Grow up	Become an adult
Hand in	Submit
Hang on	Wait for a short time
Hang up	End a phone call
Let down	Fail to support
Look after	Take care of
Look for	Try to find
Make up	Forgive each other
Pass away	Die
Pass out	Faint
Pay for	Be punished for something
Put off	Postpone
Run into	Meet unexpectedly
Run out	Have none left
Set up	Arrange
Sleep over	Stay somewhere for the night
Sort out	Resolve a problem
Take after	Resemble someone
Take off	Start to fly
Think over	Consider
Turn down	Refuse
Turn up	Appear suddenly
Wear off	Fade
Work out	Exercise

Types of Phrasal Verbs

Type 1: Verb + Adverb (with no object)
In this type, the verb and adverb cannot be separated.

Examples:
Cut back, end up, go off, run out.
We have <u>run out</u> of eggs. (Correct)
We have <u>run eggs</u> out. (Incorrect)

Type 2: Verb + Adverb + Object OR Verb + Object + Adverb
Examples:
- Find out, give away, put off, try on
  Examples:
  If the object is a noun, the adverb can go before the noun:
  She wants to <u>try on</u> the dress.

- If the object is a noun, the adverb can go after the noun:
  She wants to <u>try</u> the dress <u>on</u>.

> **TRIVIA**
> The shortest "-ology" is oology, which is the study of birds' eggs.

- If the object is a pronoun (it, them, her etc), the verb + adverb cannot be separated, the adverb comes after the object:
  Examples:
  She wants <u>to try</u> it <u>on</u>. (Correct)
  She wants <u>to try on</u> it. (Incorrect)
  It is important to practise understanding and using Phrasal verbs.

- Sometimes an alternative to the phrasal verb may sound too formal:
  Examples:
  put down (make someone feel inferior)
  The teacher likes making the students feel inferior. (Too formal)
  The teacher likes putting the students down. (Informal)

Type 3: Verb + Preposition + Object
Examples:
break into, pick on, turn into, get over
With this type of phrasal verbs in English Grammar, it is not possible to separate the preposition from the verb.
John picked on little Mary.   (Correct)
John picked on her.   (Correct)
John picked little Mary on.   (Incorrect)
John picked her on.   (Incorrect)

Type 4: Verb + Adverb + Preposition + Object
Examples:
Put up with, do away with, come out in, come up against
(The phrasal verbs in this category have two particles. They cannot be separated from the verb.)
The government wants to do away with tax on children's food.
She can't put up with the students arriving late to class.
She can't put up with them arriving late to class.

➡ Phrasal verbs are formed when a verb is followed by another word which is known as a participle.

PRACTICE EXERCISE

I. Choose the correct phrasal verbs to fill in the blanks in the following sentences.

1. I _____ but nobody has seen my wallet.
   (a) asked around (b) asked everyone
   (c) asked in (d) asked out

2. You'll have to run faster than that if you want to _____ with Marty.
   (a) catch on (b) catch up
   (c) catch (d) catch ahead

3. I don't feel like cooking tonight. Let's _____.
   (a) eat in (b) eat along
   (c) eat up (d) eat out

4. I am not being able to _____ his intentions.
   (a) figure up (b) figure out
   (c) figure in (d) figure of

5. The two brothers don't _____ with each other much.
   (a) get set (b) get well
   (c) get along (d) get going

6. The spider taught Robert Bruce to never _____.
   (a) give up (b) give away
   (c) give out (d) give in

7. _____! I'll be there with you soon.
   (a) Hang up (b) Hang there
   (c) Hanging (d) Hang on

8. Sam and Clara's wedding has been _____ for a few days.
   (a) called off (b) given off
   (c) set off (d) put off

9. I am planning to have a _____ at my place soon.
   (a) sleep in (b) sleep over
   (c) sleep under (d) sleep well

10. The twins have _____ their mother more than their father.
    (a) taken after (b) taken to
    (c) taken in (d) taken out

11. Don't make a hasty decision. _____ and get back.
    (a) get over (b) Sleep over
    (c) Think over (d) Fall over

12. Jim likes to _____ in the gym after a hard day's work.
    (a) work (b) work out
    (c) work hard (d) work along

13. How will I bake the cake? We have _____ of sugar.
    (a) run in (b) run off
    (c) run out (d) run along

14. You will _____ your mistakes one way or the other.
    (a) pay for (b) pay off
    (c) pay in (d) pay out

15. The teacher gave the last warning to the students to _____ their projects.
    (a) hands up (b) hand in
    (c) hand shake (d) hand out

II. Choose the correct options which expresses the phrasal verb given in the following questions.

1. Add up to something
   (a) Equal
   (b) Solve a math problem
   (c) A cooking term
   (d) Match something

2. Break down
   (a) Fall into pieces
   (b) Break open
   (c) Stop functioning
   (d) End relationship

3. Call off
   (a) Yell
   (b) To telephone someone
   (c) Call a meeting
   (d) Cancel

4. Chip in
   (a) Computer term (b) Help
   (c) Break (d) A type of snacks

5. Count on
   (a) Add up (b) Rely
   (c) Wait (d) Add on

6. Go ahead
   (a) Start (b) Overtake
   (c) Overcome (d) Go first

7. Let down
   (a) Lower something
   (b) Let something flow
   (c) Fail to support
   (d) Allow
8. Pass out
   (a) Die   (b) Faint
   (c) Get good marks   (d) Fail
9. Set up
   (a) Arrange   (b) Plot
   (c) Plan   (d) Revenge
10. Take off
    (a) Go away
    (b) Accept something
    (c) Take away
    (d) Start to fly
11. Turn down
    (a) Lower   (b) Refuse
    (c) Go downhill   (d) Turn sides
12. Wear off
    (a) Wear clothes   (b) Wear shoes
    (c) Fade   (d) Tear
13. Sort out
    (a) Arrange
    (b) Rearrange
    (c) Put in line
    (d) Resolve a problem
14. Make up
    (a) Paint your face
    (b) Forgive each other
    (c) Make a cake
    (d) Create something
15. Get back
    (a) Return
    (b) Give back
    (c) Find lost property
    (d) Get something

HOTS

Choose the correct phrasal verb from the list given below to replace the words underlined and change their form where necessary. There could be an extra phrasal verb:

1. (i) I cannot <u>understand</u> what he says.
   (ii) I <u>met</u> my friend in the park.
   (iii) She failed to <u>appear</u> in time.
   (iv) The strike was <u>withdrawn</u> at last.

   List: take after, call off, make out, turn up, come across.

2. (i) The girl <u>resembles</u> her mother.
   (ii) Evening <u>starts</u> early in winter.
   (iii) Our school <u>closes</u> at 4:30 pm.
   (iv) The school magazine will be <u>published</u> soon.

   List: take after, put away, breaks up, brought out, sets in.

3. (i) How could you <u>tolerate</u> such rude words?
   (ii) The girls <u>continued</u> practising the song.
   (iii) The boy <u>resembles</u> his father.
   (iv) The great leader <u>died</u> last week.

   List: look after, set in, bring out, take after, break up.

4. (i) The patient will <u>recover</u> soon.
   (ii) The police <u>chased</u> the robbers.
   (iii) One cannot <u>change</u> an old habit easily.
   (iv) The burglars <u>forcibly entered</u> the house.

   List: run after, break into, give up, get over, come round

5. (i) The army finally <u>surrendered</u>.
   (ii) The man <u>rejected</u> our proposal.
   (iii) You will soon <u>overcome</u> your problems.
   (iv) No one can <u>tolerate</u> such bad manners.

   List: stand against, get over, turn down, give in, put up with

Punctuations

Learning Objectives : In this chapter, students will learn about:
- ✓ Basic concepts of Punctuation
- ✓ Common Punctuation marks

CHAPTER SUMMARY

Punctuations are symbols used to indicate stops and pauses in a sentence. They help make our writing organized and structured.

Punctuations may be divided into two categories:

(i) The punctuations that represent stops or pause. This category includes full-stop, comma, semi-colon, colon, question mark and exclamation mark.

(ii) The punctuations that do not represent stops or pause. This category includes apostrophe, quotation mark and the hyphen.

Fullstop or Period (.)

The fullstop marks a break or end of thought. It is used to express complete sentences.

Examples:
I like to spend time with my family.
New Delhi is my favourite city.

Fullstops are also used to indicate abbreviations.

Examples:
M.P. (Member of Parliament)
S.K. Majumdar (Swapan Kumar Majumdar)

Question Mark (?)

This symbol is used to ask a direct question.

Examples:
What is the price of this phone?
Why do you look upset?

Comma (,)

(i) The comma is used to indicate pause, but it does not finish a sentence. It shows a little pause in speech or writing.

Examples:
This is my friend, John.
The team, which recreated the 70s theme, won the competition.

(ii) It is used to separate items in a list of things.

Examples:
I love to eat apples, oranges, grapes and watermelon.
My sister is good at singing, dancing, painting and cooking.
A young, handsome man drove a red, sleek car.

> **TRIVIA**
> If we place a comma before the word "and" at the end of a list, this is known as an "Oxford comma" or a "serial comma". For example: "I drink coffee, tea, and juice."

Semi-Colon (;)

The semi colon is used somewhere between a comma and a full-stop. Although it does not suggest the end of a sentence, it indicates a greater pause than a comma. It connects two different thoughts. It is used when the idea contained in the second part of the sentence is a continuation from the first, but both can stand independently as well.

Examples:
He heard a knock at the door; he went to open it.
He worked hard; he did well in the exams.

Colon (:)
The colon indicates a more complete pause than a semi colon. It is used to introduce a list, an explanation or a quotation.
Examples:
He wanted to see three cities in Italy: Rome, Florence and Venice. (list)
You can come pick me up now: I am feeling much better. (explanation)
She kept repeating: "I really want that dress!" (quotation)

Exclamation Mark (!)
The exclamation mark is used at the end of an exclamatory sentence.
Examples:
Look at the car such a beauty!
Oh! What a pity!

Apostrophe (')
The apostrophe is used to show possession.
Examples:
We add 's' when the noun is singular.
Natasha's book (singular)
My father's office (singular)
We use only the apostrophe (') for plurals.
The boys' team (plural)
The twins' room (plural)
However, we use 's' with plurals not ending with 's'.
children's corner
men's fashion

Quotation Mark ('')
The quotation mark is used to enclose speech or actual words. It is also used to enclose titles of book, movies, etc.
Examples:
He said: "I am trying my best."
"Merchant of Venice"
"Jurassic Park"

Hyphen (-)
The hyphen is used to form compound words.
Examples:
merry-go-round
daughter-in-law
one-third

MUST REMEMBER

- Punctuations are symbols used to indicate stops and pauses in a sentence.
- The fullstop marks a break or end of thought. It is used to express complete sentences.
- The comma is used to indicate pause, but it does not finish a sentence.
- The semi colon is used somewhere between a comma and a full-stop.
- It is used when the idea contained in the second part of the sentence is a continuation from the first, but both can stand independently as well.
- The colon indicates a more complete pause than a semi colon. It is used to introduce a list, an explanation or a quotation.

PRACTICE EXERCISE

I. Choose the sentence which is correctly punctuated.

1. (a) The python caught yesterday measures 21 feet.
   (b) The python, caught yesterday, measures 21 feet.
   (c) The python, caught yesterday measures 21 feet.
   (d) The python caught yesterday, measures 21 feet.

2. (a) My shirt is green, white, and blue.
   (b) My shirt is green, white and blue.
   (c) My shirt is green white, and blue.
   (d) My shirt is green white and blue.

3. (a) Arvind was born on October 18, 2004.
   (b) Arvind was born on October, 18 2004
   (c) Arvind was born on October 18 2004
   (d) Arvind was born on October 18, 2004

4. (a) Steve, the caretaker opened the door for us.
   (b) Steve the caretaker opened the door for us.
   (c) Steve, the caretaker, opened the door for us.
   (d) Steve the caretaker, opened the door for us.

5. (a) The shop, on the corner sells notebooks and paper.
   (b) The shop on the corner sells notebooks, and paper.
   (c) The shop on the corner, sells notebooks and paper.
   (d) The shop on the corner sells notebooks and paper.

6. (a) Look how beautiful the moon is.
   (b) Look how beautiful the Moon is:
   (c) Look! How beautiful the Moon is.
   (d) Look how beautiful, the moon is.

7. (a) What time does the class start?
   (b) What time does the class start
   (c) What time does the class start.
   (d) What time does the class start!

8. (a) I suggest that you read Shakespeares Macbeth.
   (b) I suggest that you read Shakespeare's "Macbeth".
   (c) I suggest that you read shakespeares macbeth.
   (d) I suggest that you read, Shakespeare's Macbeth.

9. (a) Never forget this point: Think before you speak.
   (b) Never forget this point, Think before you speak.
   (c) Never forget this point; Think before you speak.
   (d) Never forget this point. Think before you speak.

10. (a) There was a knock on the door he went to open it.
    (b) There was a knock on the door; he went to open it.
    (c) There was a knock on the door, he went to open it.
    (d) There was a knock on the door? he went to open it.

11. (a) You are coming aren't you?
    (b) You are coming aren't you!
    (c) You are coming aren't you.
    (d) You are coming, aren't you?

12. (a) Red is my favourite color I like wearing blue sometimes.
    (b) Red is my favourite color I like, wearing blue sometimes.
    (c) Red is my favourite color, I like wearing blue sometimes.
    (d) Red is my favourite color; I like wearing blue sometimes.

13. (a) I love healthy food: nuts, fruits, and vegetables.
    (b) I love healthy food nuts, fruits, and vegetables.
    (c) I love healthy food nuts fruits and vegetables.
    (d) I love healthy, food nuts, fruits, and vegetables.

14. (a) My brothers car is parked in front of the house.
    (b) My brother's car is parked in front of the house.
    (c) My brothers car, is parked in front of the house.
    (d) My brothers car is parked, in front, of the house.

Punctuations

15. (a) I don't sleep well at night I'm always tired during the day.
    (b) I don't sleep well at night, I'm always tired, during the day.
    (c) I don't sleep well at night. I'm always tired during the day.
    (d) I don't sleep well at night; I'm always tired during the day.
16. (a) The weather is hot; humidity is high.
    (b) The weather is hot humidity is high.
    (c) The weather is hot; humidity is high
    (d) The weather is hot humidity is high;
17. (a) He suddenly shouted to me, Look!
    (b) He suddenly shouted to me. "Look!"
    (c) He suddenly shouted to me, "Look!"
    (d) He suddenly shouted to me! "Look!"
18. (a) Your son plays a few games badminton, football and tennis.
    (b) Your son plays a few games: badminton football and tennis.
    (c) Your son plays a few games.badminton, football and tennis.
    (d) Your son plays a few games: badminton, football and tennis.
19. (a) I am going to receive my mother in law from the station.
    (b) I am going to receive my mother-in-law from the station.
    (c) I am going to receive my mother in law from the station
    (d) I am going to receive, my mother in law, from the station.
20. (a) I am on my way to my friends house.
    (b) I am on my way to my friend's house.
    (c) I am on my way to my friends' house.
    (d) I am on my way to my "friends" house.
21. (a) Some women, who were superstitious, did not attend the ceremony.
    (b) Some women who were superstitious did not attend the ceremony.
    (c) Some women who were superstitious did not attend the ceremony.
    (d) Some women, who were superstitious, did not attend, the ceremony.
22. (a) Meet Mark. He is the editor-in-chief.
    (b) Meet Mark. He is the editor-in chief.
    (c) Meet Mark. He is the editorinchief.
    (d) Meet Mark. He is the editor in chief.
23. (a) Do you know how to get there.
    (b) Do you know how to get there!
    (c) Do you know how to get there?
    (d) Do you know how to get there
24. (a) Speech is silver. silence is golden.
    (b) Speech is silver silence is golden.
    (c) Speech is silver-silence is golden.
    (d) Speech is silver; silence is golden.
25. (a) "Listen up everyone," the class monitor yelled.
    (b) Listen up everyone, the class monitor yelled.
    (c) "Listen up everyone, the class monitor yelled."
    (d) "Listen up everyone," "the class monitor yelled".

HOTS

Correct the punctuation in following sentences

1. the lady is wearing golden stretch pants green eyelids and a hives shaped wig
2. then lady will dress up to go shopping water the plants empty the dustbin answer the phone read a book and get the letters from the box
3. your father has five items in his bathroom a toothbrush shaving cream a razor a bar of soap and a towel
4. hurling has been the national sport of Ireland
5. we wrote the homonyms too to see sea in our notebooks.

Tenses   11

Learning Objectives : In this chapter, students will learn about:
- Basic concepts of Tenses
- Types of Tenses

CHAPTER SUMMARY

Tense is an effect of time on verb. It indicates the time when an action, a situation or an event takes place. There are three main types of tenses: present (now), past (before now) and future (after now).

Present Tense

Simple Present Tense
Simple present tense is used for actions that happen on a regular basis.

Examples:

The boy **runs** very fast.

Mr. Roy **drives** his new car to office every day.

Present Continuous Tense
The present continuous tense is used for an action that is still going on.

Examples:

I am **reading** Chetan Bhagat's new book.

The speech is **being delivered** in the hall.

Present Perfect Tense
The present perfect tense is used for an action that is completed just now.

Examples:

I **have** just **finished** my homework.

They **have paid** the price of the purchased article.

Past Tense

Simple Past Tense
Simple past tense is used for an action or event that has already happened at certain or uncertain point of time. It is usually accompanied by words such as yesterday, a week ago, last month, last year, etc.

Examples:

I **completed** my project on time last week.

Yesterday, we **went** to the zoo.

Past Continuous Tense
The past continuous tense is used for an action that went on for some time in the past.

Examples:

They **were waiting** for you all afternoon.

The boys **were playing** badminton, while the girls were dancing.

> **TRIVIA**
>
> Some words exist only in plural form, for example: glasses (spectacles), binoculars, scissors, shears, tongs, gallows, trousers, jeans, pants, etc.

Past Perfect Tense
The past perfect tense is used for an action/event that occurred before certain point of time in the past.

Examples:

We **had finished** our work before the teacher arrived .

John **had gone out** when I arrived in the office.

I **had saved** the document before the computer crashed.

Past Perfect Continuous Tense

The past perfect continuous tense is used for an action that began in the past and continued up to a point.

Examples:

It **had been raining** hard for several hours.

Had you been waiting long before the taxi arrived?

Future Form

Simple Future

Simple future form is used to denote an action that will take place in future. Usually the helping verbs 'shall' or 'will' are used with this form.

Examples:

I do not have time today, I **will meet** you tomorrow.

I **shall study** for my exam tonight.

Future Continuous

It is used to express a continued or an ongoing action in future. For example, "I **will be waiting** for you tomorrow", it conveys ongoing nature of an action (waiting) which will occur in future.

- **Rules:** Auxiliary verb "will be" is used in sentence. 1st form of verb + ing (present participle) is used as main verb in sentence.

Formation of future continuous

Positive sentence

Subject + will be+ 1st form of verb or base form+ing (present participle) + object

Examples:

I will be waiting for you.

You will be feeling well tomorrow.

Future Perfect

The future perfect form is used for an action that will be completed by a certain time in future.

Example:

I **shall have completed** revision of all chapters by next week.

I **will have left** for home by the time he wakes up.

- Simple present tense is used for actions that happen on a regular basis.
- The present continuous tense is used for an action that is still going on.
- The present perfect tense is used for an action that is completed just now.
- Simple past tense is used for an action or event that has already happened at certain or uncertain point of time.
- The past continuous tense is used for an action that went on for some time in the past.
- The past perfect tense is used for an action/event that occurred before certain point of time in the past.

PRACTICE EXERCISE

I. Choose the correct option to fill in the blanks with the correct form of verb.

1. The plane _____ at 6:30.
   (a) arrives (b) arrive
   (c) will arrive (d) arrived

2. Stars _____ brightly in the night sky.
   (a) shines (b) shining
   (c) shine (d) will shine

3. Janne _____ eight hours a day.
   (a) work (b) works
   (c) worked (d) is working

4. My sister _____ very fast.
   (a) talks (b) will talk
   (c) is talking (d) talked

5. My brother and I _____ Japanese.
   (a) speaks (b) are speaking
   (c) spoke (d) speak

II. Choose the correct option to fill in the blanks with the correct form of verb/tense.

1. Mr. Dan _____ diligently in his factory for five years.
   (a) works (b) worked
   (c) is working (d) work

2. He _____ from London yesterday.
   (a) returned (b) will return
   (c) is returning (d) returns

3. He _____ ill for a long time.
   (a) has been (b) had been
   (c) was (d) is

4. The teacher _____ us a frightening story.
   (a) will tell (b) is telling
   (c) tells (d) told

5. I _____ my grandparents last week.
   (a) visit (b) will visit
   (c) visited (d) visiting

III. Choose the correct option to fill in the blanks with the correct form of verb/future form.

1. He _____ you tonight after work.
   (a) calls (b) will call
   (c) is calling (d) called

2. The children _____ the candy.
   (a) like (b) liked
   (c) will like (d) likes

3. Class _____ at 10:30 am.
   (a) will begin (b) begins
   (c) began (d) is beginning

4. We are _____ a play at the city centre.
   (a) going to watch (b) will watch
   (c) watching (d) watched

5. I _____ you move your things tomorrow.
   (a) help (b) am helping
   (c) helped (d) will help

IV. Choose the correct option to fill in the blanks with the correct form of verb/continuous tense indicated in the bracket.

1. Hurry up! We are _____ for you. (Present)
   (a) waiting (b) waited
   (c) will wait (d) wait

2. I _____ all day yesterday. (Past)
   (a) painted (b) was painting
   (c) will paint (d) paints

3. He is _____ for Australia. (Present)
   (a) left (b) will leave
   (c) leaving (d) had left

4. They _____ the whole time they were together. (Past)
   (a) quarreled
   (b) were quarrelling
   (c) will quarrel
   (d) had quarreled

5. He is always _____ in class. (Present)
   (a) slept
   (b) sleeps
   (c) had been sleeping
   (d) sleeping

6. It happened while I _____ in London last year. (Past)
   (a) lived (b) had lived
   (c) was living (d) will live

7. The universe _____ and has been since its beginning. (Present)
   (a) expands (b) is expanding
   (c) expanded (d) had expanded

Tenses

8. The phone rang while I _____ dinner. (Past)
   (a) was having (b) had
   (c) will have (d) going to have
9. I _____ letters to my cousins. (Present)
   (a) am writing (b) will write
   (c) have written (d) wrote
10. The doctor _____ the child. (Past)
    (a) examined (b) will examine
    (c) had examined (d) was examining

V. **Choose the correct option to fill in the blanks with the correct form of verb.**

1. By the time I arrived at the bus stop, the bus _____. (Past)
   (a) left (b) had left
   (c) was leaving (d) leaves
2. By this time next year, Nancy _____ to a new apartment. (Future)
   (a) moved
   (b) will move
   (c) will have moved
   (d) is moving
3. The office _____ to a new location. (Present)
   (a) just moved (b) is moving
   (c) moved (d) will move
4. I _____ to Europe before my vacation to Spain. (Past)
   (a) went (b) will go
   (c) am going (d) had gone
5. By the time we reach Mumbai, we _____ for 10 hours. (Future)
   (a) will drive
   (b) will have driven
   (c) are driving
   (d) drove

HOTS

I. **Change the following sentences into negative:**
   1. Vishal was living in Kolkata in July last year.
   2. Vimal was talking to Vijay at ten o'clock last night.
   3. At four o'clock yesterday we were all drinking tea.
   4. I was trying to get a taxi at ten o clock last night.
   5. It was raining in Chennai at five o'clock last evening.

II. **Change the following sentences into questions:**
   1. They were crying there.
   2. He was playing cricket.
   3. He was doing his homework.
   4. Yes, Ruchi and Rubi were cooking in the kitchen.
   5. We were going to the market.

Voice

Learning Objectives : In this chapter, students will learn about:
- Basic concept of Voice
- Kinds of voice
- Rules for changing Voice

CHAPTER SUMMARY

Voice is the form of verb which expresses whether the person or thing denoted by the subject does something or something is done to it.

Examples:

Raman writes a letter to the editor of the newspaper.

(Here, the subject 'Raman' is doing an action of writing.)

A letter is written to the editor of the newspaper by Raman.

(Here, the subject 'Letter' is written by Raman.)

Kinds of Voices

There are two kinds of voices: Active Voice and Passive Voice

Sentence 1: The black dog chased the tall man. (Active Voice)

Sentence 2: The tall man was chased by the dog. (Passive Voice)

(Both these sentences mean the same thing but have been written differently.

Sentence 1 emphasizes '**who/subject**' is performing the action (the dog chases), while

Sentence 2 emphasizes who is being acted upon (the man is chased).

Therefore, Sentence 1 is in **active voice** whereas Sentence 2 is in **passive voice**.

Examples:

Alice is washing the dishes. (Active)

The dishes are being washed by Alice. (Passive)

We see films in a cinema. (Active)

Films are shown in a cinema. (Passive)

Fundamental Rules of Changing Voice

1. The places of subject and object in a sentence are interchanged while changing the voice.
2. 3rd form of verb (past participle) is used only (as main verb) in passive voice.
3. Auxiliary verbs are used as per the rules of auxiliaries in passive voice.

Note:

Intransitive verb cannot be changed into passive voice

The sentences having intransitive verbs (belonging to any tense) cannot be changed into passive voice. The reason is that there is not any object in such sentences and without object of sentence, passive voice is not possible.

A sentence can be changed into passive voice if it has subject and object. Sometimes subject may not be written in passive voice but it does not mean that it has no subject. Such sentences have subject but the subject is so common or familiar or known that if even it is not written in passive voice, it gives full meaning.

For example:

Cloth is sold in yards.

Rules of Passive Voice

1. The places of subject and object are interchanged in transformation of voices.

2. 3rd form of verb (past participle) is used only in passive voice.
3. Auxiliary verbs are used according to tenses.

> The "QWERTY keyboard" gains its name from the fact that its first 6 letter keys are Q, W, E, R, T and Y.

Present Simple Tense
Auxiliary verb in passive voice: **am/is/are**

Examples:

He sings a song. (Active voice)

A song is sung by him. (Passive voice)

Present Continuous Tense
Auxiliary verb in passive voice: **am being/is being/are being**

Examples:

I am writing a letter. (Active voice)

A letter is being written by me. (Passive voice)

Am I writing a letter? (Active voice)

Is a letter being written by me? (Passive voice)

Present Perfect Tense
Auxiliary verb in passive voice: **has been/have been**

Examples:

She has finished her work. (Active voice)

Her work has been finished by her. (Passive voice)

Has she finished her work? (Active voice)

Has her work been finished by her? (Passive voice)

Past Simple Tense
Auxiliary verb in passive voice: **was/were**

Examples:

I did not kill a snake. (Active voice)

A snake was not killed by me. (Passive voice)

Did I kill a snake? (Active voice)

Was a snake killed by me? (Passive voice)

Past Continuous Tense
Auxiliary verb in passive voice: **was being/were being**

Examples:

He was driving a car. (Active voice)

A car was being driven by him. (Passive voice)

Was he driving a car? (Active voice)

Was a car being driven by him? (Passive voice)

Past Perfect Tense
Auxiliary verb in passive voice: **had been**

Examples:

They had completed the assignment. (Active voice)

The assignment had been completed by them. (Passive voice)

Had they completed the assignment? (Active voice)

Had the assignment been completed by them? (Passive voice)

Future Simple Form
Auxiliary verb in passive voice: **will be**

Examples:

She will buy a car. (Active voice)

A car will be bought by her. (Passive voice)

Will she buy a car? (Active voice)

Will a car be bought by her? (Passive voice)

Future Perfect Form
Auxiliary verb in passive voice: **will have been**

Examples:

You will not have started the job. (Active voice)

The job will not have been started by you. (Passive voice)

Will you have started the job? (Active voice)

Will the job have been started by you? (Passive voice)

Note:
The following tenses cannot be changed into passive voice.
1. Present perfect continuous tense
2. Past perfect continuous tense
3. Future continuous form
4. Future perfect continuous form
5. Sentence having Intransitive verbs

Passive Voice of Imperative Sentences

A sentence which expresses command or request or advice is called imperative sentence. For changing these sentences into passive voice, auxiliary verb 'be' is used. The word 'let' is added before sentence in passive voice. Auxiliary verb 'be' is added after object in sentence in passive voice. Main verb (base form) of imperative sentence is changed to 3rd form of verb (past participle) in passive voice.

Examples:

Open the door. (Active Voice)
Let the door be opened. (Passive Voice)
Turn off the television. (Active Voice)
Let the television be turned off. (Passive Voice)
Learn your lesson. (Active Voice)
Let your lesson be learnt. (Passive Voice)
Speak the truth. (Active Voice)
Let the truth be spoken. (Passive Voice)
Revise your book. (Active Voice)
Let your book be revised. (Passive Voice)
Clean your room. (Active Voice)
Let your room be cleaned. (Passive Voice)

MUST REMEMBER

- Voice is the form of verb which expresses whether the person or thing denoted by the subject does something or something is done to it.
- The sentences having intransitive verbs cannot be changed into passive voice.
- A sentence can be changed into passive voice if it has subject and object.
- The following tenses cannot be changed into passive voice.
    1. Present perfect continuous tense
    2. Past perfect continuous tense
    3. Future continuous form
    4. Future perfect continuous form
    5. Sentence having Intransitive verbs
- A sentence which expresses command or request or advice is called imperative sentence.

PRACTICE EXERCISE

I. **Choose the sentence which is given in active voice.**

1. (a) Beautiful giraffes roam the savannah forest.
   (b) The savannah is roamed by beautiful girraffes.
   (c) The savannahs are roamed by beautiful girraffes.
   (d) None of these

2. (a) Harry ate six pancakes at dinner.
   (b) At dinner, six pancakes were eaten by Harry.
   (c) At dinner, six pancakes are eaten by Harry.
   (d) None of these

3. (a) Sue changed the flat tire.
   (b) The flat tire was changed by Sue.
   (c) The flat tire had changed by Sue.
   (d) None of these

4. (a) A movie is going to be watched by us tonight.
   (b) We are going to watch a movie tonight.
   (c) We are going watch a movie tonight.
   (d) None of these

5. (a) He liked to his students.
   (b) He is liked by his students.
   (c) His students like him.
   (d) None of these

6. (a) I ran the obstacle course in record time.
   (b) The obstacle course was run by me in record time.
   (c) The obstacle course had run by me in record time.
   (d) None of these

7. (a) The entire stretch of highway paved to the crew.
   (b) The entire stretch of highway was paved by the crew.
   (c) The crew paved the entire stretch of highway.
   (d) None of these

8. (a) The novel was read by Mom in one day.
   (b) Mom read the novel in one day.
   (c) Mom has readed the novel in one day.
   (d) None of these

9. (a) He threw the plastic bottles into the crate.
   (b) The plastic bottles were thrown into the crate by him.
   (c) The plastic bottles were thrown in the crate by him.
   (d) None of these

10. (a) The house will be cleaned by me every Saturday.
    (b) I will clean the house every Saturday.
    (c) I will cleaned the house every Saturday.
    (d) None of these

11. (a) She faxed the application for a new job.
    (b) The application for a new job was faxed by her.
    (c) The application for a new job was faxed by her.
    (d) The application for a new job was faxed by her.

12. (a) The entire house was painted by Tom.
    (b) Tom painted the entire house.
    (c) Tom painting the entire house.
    (d) None of these

13. (a) A procession will be hold by them next week.
    (b) A procession will be held by them next week.
    (c) They will hold a procession next week.
    (d) None of these

14. (a) Who taught you to ski?
    (b) By whom were you taught to ski?
    (c) Whom were you taught to ski?
    (d) None of these

15. (a) The whole suburb was destroyed by the forest fire.
    (b) The forest fire destroyed the whole suburb.
    (c) The forest fire destroying the whole suburb.
    (d) None of these

II. **Choose the sentence which is given in passive voice.**

1. (a) The video was posted on Facebook by Alex.
   (b) Alex posted the video on Facebook.
   (c) Alex has posted the video on Facebook.
   (d) None of these

2. (a) He removed all the evidence.
   (b) All the evidence was removed by him.
   (c) He removed all the evidence.
   (d) None of these
3. (a) You can't blame them.
   (b) They can't be blamed.
   (c) They was't be blamed.
   (d) None of these
4. (a) The team will celebrate their victory tomorrow.
   (b) The victory will be celebrated by the team tomorrow.
   (c) The victory shall be celebrated by the team tomorrow.
   (d) None of these
5. (a) The dishes were washed by John.
   (b) John washed the dishes.
   (c) John wash the dish.
   (d) None of these
6. (a) They were distributing pamphlets.
   (b) Pamphlets is being distributed by them.
   (c) Pamphlets are being distributed by them.
   (d) None of these
7. (a) Larry donated money to the homeless shelter generously.
   (b) Money was generously donated to the homeless shelter by Larry.
   (c) Money were generously donated to the homeless shelter by Larry.
   (d) None of these
8. (a) They occupied the front seats.
   (b) The front seats were occupied by them.
   (c) The front seats was occupied by them.
   (d) None of these
9. (a) The wedding planner will make all the reservations.
   (b) All the reservations will be made by the wedding planner.
   (c) All the reservations shall be made by the wedding planner.
   (d) None of these
10. (a) Susan will bake two dozen cookies for the bake sale.
    (b) For the bake sale, two dozen cookies shall be baked by Susan.
    (c) For the bake sale, two dozen cookies will be baked by Susan.
    (d) None of these
11. (a) The last cookie was eaten by whom?
    (b) Who ate the last cookie?
    (c) Who eat the last cookie?
    (d) None of these
12. (a) The kangaroo carried her baby in her pouch.
    (b) The baby was carried by the kangaroo in her pouch.
    (c) The baby were carried by the kangaroo in her pouch.
    (d) None of these
13. (a) My sales ad was not responded to by anyone.
    (b) No one responded to my sales ad.
    (c) No one respond to my sales ad.
    (d) None of these
14. (a) The director will give you instructions.
    (b) Instructions will be given to you by the director.
    (c) Instructions shall be given to you by the director.
    (d) None of these
15. (a) She has burnt the toast again.
    (b) The toast has been burnt by her again.
    (c) The toast had been burnt by her again.
    (d) None of these

Voice

HOTS

I. Choose the correct active/passive voice of the given sentence.

1. Shivu is singing a song.
   (a) A song has been being sung by Shivu.
   (b) A song is sung by Shivu.
   (c) A song has being sung by Shivu.
   (d) A song is being sung by Shivu.
2. My friends are watching the match.
   (a) The match is watched by my friends.
   (b) The match had being watched by my friends.
   (c) The match is being watched by my friends.
   (d) The match has being watched by my friends.
3. He can speak French.
   (a) French can spoken by him.
   (b) French can be spoke by him.
   (c) French can be spoken by him.
   (d) French could be spoken by him.
4. They may win the battle.
   (a) The battle may be win.
   (b) The battle may be won.
   (c) The battle may be won by them.
   (d) The battle may won.
5. Nobody can catch him.
   (a) He cannot be caught.
   (b) He can not caught.
   (c) He could not be cought.
   (d) He could not cought.

II. Read the statements given below and chose the correct option.

1. Identify the Passive Voice :
   (a) Reena sings a song.
   (b) The students were making a chart.
   (c) She lost the match.
   (d) A mistake was made by her.
2. Identify the Passive Voice :
   (a) A song is sung by Lata.
   (b) He bought the pens.
   (c) They study the book.
   (d) Lalit killed the snake.
3. Identify the Active Voice :
   (a) The rumour has been spread.
   (b) The ship had been broken.
   (c) Why did the teacher punish you?
   (d) The noise was made by the class.
4. Identify the Active Voice :
   (a) The letter has been posted.
   (b) The thief was arrested.
   (c) The song was sung.
   (d) They lost everything.
5. Fill in the object:
   He ran a _____
   (a) scooter   (b) race
   (c) fight   (d) building

Narration 13

Learning Objectives : In this chapter, students will learn about:
- ✓ Concept of Narration
- ✓ Direct and Indirect Speech

CHAPTER SUMMARY

Narration means the way we tell a story, or something that we have heard from someone else. In grammar, the manner of expressing the words of speaker is called narration. The words of speaker can be expressed in two ways: direct and indirect.

Example:
We can either use the exact words of the speaker, called direct speech.

Rohan said, "I have written a letter."(Direct speech)

We can use our own words to convey the exact same message called indirect speech.

Example:
Rohan said that he had written a letter. (Indirect speech)

Direct Speech

Direct speech repeats, or quotes, the exact words spoken. When we use direct speech in writing, we place the words spoken between quotation marks (" ") and there is no change in these words.

Example:
She said, "What time will you be at home?" and I said, "I don't know!"

"There's a fly in my soup!" screamed Simone.

Marlene said to her mother, "Mom, I will be late for dinner."

Indirect Speech

The second method of speech is called indirect or reported speech.

In Indirect Speech, actual words of speaker are expressed without quotation marks.

Example:
She asked me what time I'll be at home and I said that I did not know.

Simone screamed that there was a fly in her soup.

Marlene said to her mother that she would be late for dinner.

TRIVIA

If you try to say the alphabet without moving your lips or tongue every letter will sound the same.

Rules for Changing the Narration

There are five rules for changing direct speech into indirect speech.

(i) Changing the tense of reporting verb.
(ii) Applying the connector removing comma and inverted comma.
(iii) Changing personal pronouns in reported speech.
(iv) Changing the tense of reported verb.
(v) Changing the words showing nearness.

Changing the Tense of Reported Speech

- Present simple tense → Past simple
- Present Continuous tense → Past continuous
- Present Perfect tense → Past perfect
- Present Perfect Continuous → Past perfect continuous

- Past simple → Past Perfect
- Past Continuous → Past Perfect Continuous
- Past Perfect → Past Perfect

Present Simple changes into Past Simple
Example:
She said, "he goes to school daily." (Direct Speech)
She said that he went to school daily. (Indirect Speech)
They said, "we love our country." (Direct Speech)
They said that they loved their country. (Indirect Speech)

Present Continuous changes into Past Continuous
Example:
She said, "I am washing my clothes." (Direct Speech)
She said that she was washing her clothes. Indirect Speech)
They said, "we are enjoying the weather." (Direct Speech)
They said that they were enjoying the weather. (Indirect Speech)

Present Perfect changes into Past Perfect
Example:
He said, "I have started a job." (Direct Speech)
He said that he had started a job. (Indirect Speech)
I said, "she has eaten the meal." (Direct Speech)
I said that she had eaten the meal. (Indirect Speech)

Present Perfect Continuous changes into Past Perfect Continuous
Example:
He said, "I have been studying since 3 O'clock." (Direct Speech)
He said that he had been studying since 3 O'clock. (Indirect Speech)
She said, "It has been raining for three days." (Direct Speech)
She said that it had been raining for three days. (Indirect Speech)

Past Simple changes into Past Perfect
Example:
He said to me, "you answered correctly." (Direct Speech)
He said to me that I had answered correctly. (Indirect Speech)
She said, "I didn't buy a car." (Direct Speech)
She said that she had not bought a car. (Indirect Speech)

Past Continuous changes into Past Perfect Continuous
Example:
They said, "we were enjoying the weather." (Direct Speech)
They said that they had been enjoying the weather. (Indirect Speech)
She said, "I was not laughing." (Direct Speech)
She said that she had not been laughing. (Indirect Speech)

Past Perfect changes into Past Perfect
Example:
I said, "she had eaten the meal." (Direct Speech)
I said that she had eaten the meal. (Indirect Speech)
They said, "we had not gone to New York. (Direct Speech)
They said they had not gone to New York. (Indirect Speech)

Future Simple Tense: Will changes into Would
Example:
He said, "I will study the book." (Direct Speech)
He said that he would study the book. (Indirect Speech)
They said to me, "we will send you gifts." (Direct Speech)
They said to me that they would send me gifts. (Indirect Speech)
I said, "I will not take the exam." (Direct Speech)
I said that I would not take the exam. (Indirect Speech)

Future Continuous Tense: Will be changes into Would Be
Example:
She said," I will be shifting to new home". (Direct Speech)
She said that she would be shifting to a new home. (Indirect Speech)
He said, "he will not be flying kite". (Direct Speech)

He said that he would not be flying kite. (Indirect Speech)

Future Perfect Tense: Will have changes into Would have
Example:
He said, "I will have finished the work". (Direct Speech)
He said that he would have finished the work. (Indirect Speech)
She said, "they will have passed the examination". (Direct Speech)
She said that they would have passed the examination. (Indirect Speech)

> **Note:**
> The tense of reported speech may not change if reported speech is a universal truth though its reporting verb is in past tense.
> *Example:*
> He said, "Mathematics is a science" (Direct Speech)
> He said that mathematics is a science. (Indirect Speech)
> He said, "Sun rises in east" (Direct Speech)
> He said that sun rises in east. (Indirect Speech)

Indirect Speech of Modals
- Can changes into Could
  Example:
  He said, "I can drive a car".
  He said that he could drive a car.
- May changes into Might
  Example:
  She said, "he may visit a doctor."
  She said that he might visit a doctor.
  They said, "they may go to zoo".
  They said that they might go to zoo.
- Must changes into Had to
  Example:
  She said, "they must carry on their work".
  She said that they had to carry on their work.

Indirect Speech of Modals in Past Tense
- **Would remains unchanged**
  Example:
  He said, "I would start a business.
  He said that he would start a business.
  She said, "I would appear in exam."
  She said that she would appear in the exam.
- **Could remains unchanged**
  Example:
  They said, "we couldn't learn the lesson."
  They said they couldn't learn the lesson.
- **Might remains unchanged**
  Example:
  She said, "it might rain."
  She said that it might rain.
  John said, "I might meet him."
  John said that he might meet him.
- **Should remains unchanged**
  Example:
  He said, "I should avail the opportunity."
  He said that he should avail the opportunity.
  They said, "we should take the exam."
  They said that they should take the exam.
- **Ought to remains unchanged**
  Example:
  He said to me, "you ought to wait for him."
  He said to me that I ought to wait for him.
  She said, "I ought to learn method of study."
  She said that she ought to learn method of study.

Changing the Words Showing Nearness
- *Today* → that day/the same day
- *Tomorrow* → the next day/the following day
- *Yesterday* → the day before/the previous day
- *Next week/month/year* → the following week/month/year
- *Last week/month/year* → the previous week/month/year
- *Now/just* → then
- *Ago* → before
- *Here* → there
- *This* → that

Narration

Changing Pronouns in Indirect Speech

The pronoun (subject) of the reported speech is changed according to the pronoun of reporting verb or object (person) of reporting verb (first part of sentence). Sometimes the pronoun may not change.

- First person pronoun in reported speech i.e. I, we, me, us, mine, or our, is changed according to the pronoun of reporting verb if pronoun in reporting verb is third person pronoun i.e. he, she, it, they, him, his, her, them or their.

Example:

He said, "I live in New York."(Direct speech)

He said that he lived in New York. (Indirect speech)

They said, "we love our country." (Direct speech)

They said that they loved their country. (Indirect speech)

- First person pronoun in reported speech i.e. I, we, me, us, mine, or our, is not changed if the pronoun (subject) of reporting is also first person pronoun i.e. I or we.

Example:

I said, "I write a letter." (Direct speech)

I said that I wrote a letter. (Indirect speech)

We said, "we completed our work." (Direct speech)

We said that we had completed our work. (Indirect speech)

- Second person pronoun in reported speech i.e. you, yours is changed according to the person of object of reporting verb.

Example:

She said to him, "you are intelligent." (Direct speech)

She said to him that he was intelligent. (Indirect speech)

He said to me, "you are late for the party." (Direct speech)

He said to me that I was late for the party. (Indirect speech)

- Third person pronoun in reported speech i.e. he, she, it, they, him, his, her, them or their, is not changed in indirect speech.

Example:

They said, "he will come." (Direct speech)

They said that he would come. (Indirect speech)

You said, "they are waiting for the bus." (Direct speech)

You said that they were waiting for the bus. (Indirect speech)

Indirect Speech of Imperative Sentences

A sentence which expresses command, request, advice or suggestion is called imperative sentence.

To change such sentences into indirect speech, the word 'ordered' or 'requested' or 'advised' or 'suggested' or 'forbade' or 'not to do' is added to reporting verb depending upon nature of imperative sentence in reported speech.

Example:

He said to me, "please help me." (Direct speech)

He requested me to help him. (Indirect speech)

He said to him, "you should work hard for exam." (Direct speech)

He suggested him to work hard for exam. (Indirect speech)

They said to him, "do not tell a lie." (Direct speech)

They said to him not to tell a lie. (Indirect speech)

He said, "open the door." (Direct speech)

He ordered to open the door. (Indirect speech)

The teacher said to student, "do not waste time." (Direct speech)

The teacher advised the students not to waste time. (Indirect speech)

Indirect Speech of Exclamatory Sentences

Sentence which expresses the state of joy or sorrow or wonder is called exclamatory sentence.

To change such sentences, the words "exclaimed with joy" or "exclaimed with sorrow" or "exclaimed with wonder" are added in the reporting verb depending upon the nature of exclamatory sentence in indirect speech.

Example:

He said, "Hurrah! I won a prize" (Direct speech)

He exclaimed with joy that he had won a prize. (Indirect speech)

She said, "Alas! I failed in exam" (Direct speech)

She exclaimed with sorrow that she had failed in the exam. (Indirect speech)

John said, "Wow! What a nice shirt it is" (Direct speech)

John exclaimed with wonder that it was a nice shirt. (Indirect speech)

MUST REMEMBER

- Narration means the way we tell a story, or something that we have heard from someone else.
- Direct speech repeats, or quotes, the exact words spoken.
- In Indirect Speech, actual words of speaker are expressed without quotation marks.
- **A sentence which expresses command, request, advice or suggestion is called imperative sentence.**
- Sentence which expresses the state of joy or sorrow or wonder is called exclamatory sentence.

PRACTICE EXERCISE

I. Choose the correct option that expresses direct speech.

1. (a) "He says", I have come to help you.
   (b) He says, I have come to help you.
   (c) "He says, I have come to help you."
   (d) He says, "I have come to help you."

2. (a) The mother said to her son, "Don't go near the fire."
   (b) The mother said to her son, don't go near the fire.
   (c) "The mother said to her son, don't go near the fire."
   (d) The mother said to her son to not go near the fire.

3. (a) Don't waste your money she said.
   (b) "Don't waste your money", she said.
   (c) "Don't waste" your money, she said.
   (d) She said not to waste money.

4. (a) Manu said, I am very busy now.
   (b) "Manu said I am very busy now".
   (c) Manu said, "I am very busy now".
   (d) Manu said he was busy.

5. (a) "Hurry up," she said to us.
   (b) "Hurry up, she said to us."
   (c) Hurry up, she said to us.
   (d) She asked us to hurry up.

6. (a) "Where are you going? James asked Mary."
   (b) Where are you going? James asked Mary.
   (c) "Where are you going?", James asked Mary.
   (d) James asked Mary where she was going.

7. (a) "She said to me, You are my only friend."
   (b) She said to me, You are my only friend.
   (c) She told me I was her only friend.
   (d) She said to me, "You are my only friend."

8. (a) What a lovely place this is! he said.
   (b) "What a lovely place this is! he said."
   (c) He exclaimed this was a lovely place.
   (d) "What a lovely place this is!", he said.

9. (a) "Vote for me and save the country," cried the candidate.
   (b) "Vote for me and save the country, cried the candidate."
   (c) Vote for me and save the country, cried the candidate.
   (d) The candidate asked everyone to vote for him and save the country.

10. (a) He said, I have got a toothache.
    (b) He said, "I have got a toothache".
    (c) "He said, I have got a toothache".
    (d) He said he had a toochache.

II. Choose the correct option that expresses indirect speech.

1. (a) He asked her to give him a cup of water.
   (b) "Give me a cup of water," he told her.
   (c) He asked her to give me a cup of water.
   (d) He asked her to "give him a cup of water."

2. (a) She said to me, "Thank you"
   (b) She thanked me.
   (c) She "thanked me".
   (d) She said thank you.

3. (a) He said that "he had passed the history test."
   (b) He said, "I have passed the history test."
   (c) He said that I have passed the history test.
   (d) He said that he had passed the history test.

4. (a) She requested them not to litter there.
   (b) She requested them "not to litter there."
   (c) She requested do not litter here.
   (d) She politely asked them, "Do not litter here."

5. (a) Rahul asked me, "Did you see the cricket match on TV last night?"
   (b) Rahul asked me if I had seen the cricket match on TV the previous night.
   (c) Rahul asked me did I see the cricket match on TV last night.
   (d) Rahul asked me did you see the cricket match on TV last night.

6. (a) James told his mother that he was leaving for New York the next day.
   (b) James told his mother I am leaving for New York tomorrow.
   (c) James said to his mother, "I am leaving for New York tomorrow."
   (d) James told his mother I am leaving for New York the next day.

7. (a) I said to him, "Why don't you work hard?"
    (b) I asked him why he didn't work hard.
    (c) I asked him why didn't you work hard.
    (d) I asked him why he don't you work hard?
8. (a) He said to her, "What a hot day!"
    (b) He told her what a hot day.
    (c) He exclaimed that it was a hot day.
    (d) He exclaimed to her what a hot day.
9. (a) The priest urged them to be quiet and to listen to his words.
    (b) The priest said, "Be quiet and listen to my words."
    (c) The priest said to them to be quiet and listen to my words.
    (d) The priest said them to be quiet and listen to his words.
10. (a) He asked me how you arrived at the conclusion.
    (b) He asked me, "how I arrived at the conclusion."
    (c) He asked me how did I conclude this?
    (d) He asked me how I arrived at the conclusion.

HOTS

I. **Choose the correct indirect speech of the given sentences.**

1. Robin will say to me, "I am your class-mate".
    (a) Robin will tell me that he is my classmate.
    (b) Robin will tell me that he was my classmate.
    (c) Robin will tell me that he will be my classmate.
    (d) Robin said me that he is my classmate.
2. Deepak said to me, "I had finished the coffee."
    (a) Deepak told me that he had finished the coffee.
    (b) Deepak told me that he had been finished the coffee.
    (c) Deepak told me that he had finish the coffee.
    (d) Deepak told me that he finished the coffee.
3. Rahul said to me, " I had gone through it."
    (a) Rahul told me that he have went through it.
    (b) Rahul told me that he have gone through it.
    (c) Rahul told me that he had went through it.
    (d) Rahul told me that he had gone through it.
4. Balaji said to me, "I had been working on it for 5 days."
    (a) Balaji told me that he had been working on it for 5 days.
    (b) Balaji told me that he has been working on it for 5 days.
    (c) Balaji told me that he had worked on it for 5 days.
    (d) Balaji told me that he was working on it for 5 days.
5. Sweety said to me, "I had been writing an essay for 3 hours."
    (a) Sweety told me that she has been writing an essay for 3 hours.
    (b) Sweety told me that she had been writing an essay for 3 hours.
    (c) Sweety told me that she was writing an essay for 3 hours.
    (d) Sweety told me that she had written an essay for 3 hours.

II. **Change the following sentences from Indirect to Direct speech**

1. He says that he is going to Calcutta.
2. He said that he wanted a book.
3. Ravi told his friends that they might go when they liked.
4. The teacher told me that I have not done my work well.
5. Suresh said that he had written a letter.
6. She asked me if I would go to the cinema the next day.
7. Mohan asked the postman if there was a letter for him.
8. The teacher advised the boy to work hard.
9. He requested his friend to give him his book.
10. The father advised his son not to smoke.

Spelling 14

Learning Objectives : In this chapter, students will learn about:
- Different rules of Spelling

CHAPTER SUMMARY

Knowing spelling rules is a great strategy to help you understand why spelling is important. Learning spelling rules helps you spell well. Once you learn those rules; even if you forget the rule, maybe you'll remember the spelling pattern.

Let's look at the top ten rules in a very basic way with no exceptions.

Rule 1. Keeping "**i** before **e** except after **c**" rule

Example:

believe - receive

Exception:

Ancient, leisure, neighbour/neighbor

We have a longer version of the rule:

" 'i' before 'e' except after a long 'c' but not when 'c' is a 'sh' sound and not when sounded like 'a' as in neighbour or weigh."

Example:

('i' before 'e' rule) believe, achieve, (except after 'c'), receive, ceiling (but not when 'c' is sounded like sh) ancient, proficient not when sounded like 'a') eight, beige

Rule 2. Changing 'y' to 'ies'

If the word has a consonant before the 'y', take off the 'y' and add 'ies'

Example:

baby → babies

When the word ends in a vowel followed by 'y', just add 's'.

key → keys, delay → delays, trolley → trolleys, company → companies, difficulty → difficulties

> **TRIVIA**
>
> There is a word in the English language with only one vowel, which occurs five times: "indivisibility."

Rule 3. Adding -es to words ending in -s, -ss, -z -ch -sh -x

Example:

bus → buses, business → businesses, watch → watches, box → boxes, quiz → quizzes

Rule 4. When a word has one syllable + one vowel followed by one consonant, we double the final consonant with a vowel suffix:

put–putting, big–bigger, quiz–quizzes, swim–swimming...

sit–sitter, big–biggest, tap–tapping, shop–shopper/shopping, fat–fatten, fatter, fattest...

This happens in longer words when the stress is on the final syllable:

Example:

begin (beGIN) beginner, beginning
refer (reFER) referring, referred
occur (ocCUR) occurring, occurred, occurrence

Rule 5. We usually drop the final silent 'e' when we add vowel suffix endings, for example:

Examples:

write + ing → writing
hope + ed = hoped
excite + able = excitable
large - largish
close - closing

Rule 6. We keep the 'e' if the word ends in CE or GE to keep a soft sound, with able/ous

Examples:
courage + ous = courageous
notice + able = noticeable
manage + able = manageable

Rule 7. Changing the 'y' to 'i' when adding suffix endings.

If a word ends in a consonant followed by Y, Y changes to i before adding a suffix to the word.

Examples:
beauty + ful = beauti+ful = beautiful, beautify, beautician
happy + ness = happiness, happily, happier, happiest
angry + er = angrier, angriest, angrily,
pretty: prettier, prettiest but prettyish
dry: dried, drying, dryish
defy: defies, defied, but defying
apply: applies, applied but applying

Rule 8. Most words ending in 'f' or 'fe' change their plurals to '-ves'

Examples:
half - halves
knife - knives
loaf - loaves
life - lives
thief - thieves
yourself - yourselves

Exceptions:
scarf - scarfs
dwarf - dwarfs
handkerchief - handkerchiefs

In the words ending in -ff, you just add -s to make them plural.
cliff - cliffs
scuff - scuffs
sniff - sniffs

Some words ending in 'f' add 's':
Nouns which end in two vowels followed by f, usually form plurals in the normal way, with just an -s.

- chief - chiefs, spoof - spoofs, roof - roofs, chief - chiefs, oaf - oafs

Exceptions:
thief - thieves, leaf - leaves

Rule 9. The suffix –FUL is always spelt with one L,
Examples:
grate + ful = grateful, faith + ful = faithful, hope + ful = hopeful

Rule 10. When we add -ly to words ending in -ful, we have double letters double 'll'.
Examples:
grateful + ly = gratefully, faithful + ly = faithfully, hopeful + ly = hopefully

- We also add -ly to words ending in 'e'
  love + ly = lovely, like + ly = likely, live + ly = lively
  complete + ly = completely
  definite + ly = definitely

- BUT not truly (true + ly). This is a common misspelled word.
  We change the ending 'e' to 'y' in the words ending in 'le'
  gentle = gently
  idle = idly
  subtle = subtly

Rule 11. When we add 'all' to the beginning of words, we drop one 'l'
Examples:
all + so = also
all + most = almost
although
already
alright (all right as two words is used in more formal English)
altogether (Note that altogether and all together do not mean the same thing. Altogether means 'in total', as in there are six bedrooms altogether, whereas all together means 'all in one place' or 'all at once', as in it was good to have a group of friends all together; they came in all together.)

MUST REMEMBER

➡ Knowing spelling rules is a great strategy to help you understand why spelling is important.
➡ If a word ends in a consonant followed by Y, Y changes to I before adding a suffix to the word.

Spelling

PRACTICE EXERCISE

I. Choose the correct word/option with spellings to replace the given phrase.

1. Kind and generous
   (a) benevolent   (b) benavolent
   (c) benevalent   (d) benevolent

2. Very bad or unpleasant
   (a) dispicable   (b) despecable
   (c) despicable   (d) dispecable

3. Strange or unusual
   (a) eccentric   (b) eccentric
   (c) accentric   (d) eccentrik

4. Sure to happen
   (a) enevitable   (b) inavitable
   (c) inevetable   (d) inevitable

5. Sad mood
   (a) malancholy   (b) melancoly
   (c) melancholy   (d) milancholy

6. Dull and ordinary
   (a) mundane   (b) mandane
   (c) munden   (d) mundain

7. Suggesting that something bad is going to happen in the future
   (a) aminous   (b) ominous
   (c) omminous   (d) ominus

8. No longer used
   (a) absolete   (b) obsulute
   (c) obsoleet   (d) obsolete

9. By only a small amount
   (a) scarely   (b) scarcely
   (c) scarsely   (d) scersly

10. The main character
    (a) protanagist (b) prataganist
    (c) protagonist (d) protagonest

11. To go away or escape
    (a) absconding   (b) abskonding
    (c) abconding   (d) adscanding

12. To kill or destroy by fire
    (a) emmolation   (b) emolation
    (c) imolation   (d) immolation

13. Refusing to change one's ideas or actions
    (a) stuborn   (b) stabarn
    (c) stubborn   (d) stubbarn

14. Having more than one meaning
    (a) ambigeous   (b) ambiguous
    (c) embiguous   (d) ombiguous

15. Being related to a person who lived in the past
    (a) desendent   (b) decandent
    (c) descended   (d) descendant

II. Find out the word/option incorrect spellings.

1. (a) action   (b) climete
   (c) express   (d) mammal

2. (a) temperature   (b) emergency
   (c) mith   (d) rumour

3. (a) intermision   (b) acquire
   (c) requirement   (d) vegetable

4. (a) partial   (b) pateint
   (c) unsuccessful (d) immediate

5. (a) preferable   (b) millionaire
   (c) exagerate   (d) restaurant

6. (a) violence   (b) separately
   (c) aknowledgement (d) strengthen

7. (a) desperately   (b) courageous
   (c) variety   (d) encyclopadia

8. (a) independance (b) systematic
   (c) scissors   (d) vacuum

9. (a) honourable   (b) legue
   (c) marriage   (d) ambulance

10. (a) mischievous (b) museum
    (c) rhythmic   (d) noticable

11. (a) unbelieveable (b) ingredient
    (c) headache   (d) rehearse

12. (a) grateful   (b) governor
    (c) listening   (d) lightining

13. (a) abreviation (b) applaud
    (c) choir   (d) canyon

14. (a) endurance   (b) galaxy
    (c) forhead   (d) heritage

15. (a) pledge   (b) surrounded
    (c) yeild   (d) vein

HOTS

1. In the following questions four groups of words are given. In each group one word is misspelt. Find the misspelt word.
   (a) puntuation (b) puncture
   (c) pungent (d) pudding

2. In the following questions four groups of words are given. In each group one word is misspelt. Find the misspelt word.
   (a) decency (b) promoter
   (c) deficency (d) discourteous

3. In the following questions four groups of words are given. In each group one word is misspelt. Find the misspelt word.
   (a) envelop (b) attenuate
   (c) uncertain (d) conclude

4. In the following questions four groups of words are given. In each group one word is misspelt. Find the misspelt word.
   (a) pronounse (b) enhance
   (c) performing (d) exclusion

5. In the following questions four groups of words are given. In each group one word is misspelt. Find the misspelt word.
   (a) demurrage (b) cultivat
   (c) demonstrate (d) permanent

Collocation 15

Learning Objectives : In this chapter, students will learn about:
- ✓ Basic concepts of Collocation

CHAPTER SUMMARY

Collocation is a combination of two or more words that are often used together. These combinations have been in use for many years and have become a part of natural English vocabulary.

The following is a list of some commonly used collocations.

1. **Collocations starting with the verb 'Do'**
   - Do me a favour
   - Do the cooking
   - Do your best
   - Do your hair

2. **Collocations with the verb 'Have'**
   - Have a good time
   - Have a bath
   - Have a drink
   - Have a haircut
   - Have a holiday
   - Have a problem
   - Have a relationship
   - Have lunch
   - Have sympathy

3. **Collocations with the verb 'Break'**
   - Break the law
   - Break a leg
   - Break a promise
   - Break a record
   - Break someone's heart
   - Break the ice
   - Break the news to someone
   - Break the rules

> **TRIVIA**
> The phrase "long time no see" is believed to be a literal translation of a Native American or Chinese phrase as it is not grammatically correct.

4. **Collocations with the verb 'Take'**
   - Take a break
   - Take a chance
   - Take a look
   - Take a rest
   - Take a seat
   - Take a taxi
   - Take an exam
   - Take notes
   - Take someone's place

5. **Collocations with the verb 'Make'**
   - Make a difference
   - Make a mess
   - Make a mistake
   - Make a noise
   - Make an effort
   - Make money
   - Make progress
   - Make room
   - Make trouble

6. **Collocations with the verb 'Catch'**
   - Catch the bus
   - Catch a ball
   - Catch a cold
   - Catch a thief
   - Catch fire
   - Catch sight of
   - Catch someone's attention
   - Catch someone's eye
   - Catch the flu
7. **Collocations with the verb 'Pay'**
   - Pay respect
   - Pay a fine
   - Pay attention
   - Pay by credit card
   - Pay cash
   - Pay interest
   - Pay someone a visit
   - Pay the bill
   - Pay the price
8. **Collocations with the verb 'Keep'**
   - Keep the change
   - Keep a promise
   - Keep a secret
   - Keep an appointment
   - Keep calm
   - Keep in touch
   - Keep quiet
   - Keep someone's place
9. **Collocations with the verb 'Save'**
   - Save yourself the trouble
   - Save electricity
   - Save energy
   - Save money
   - Save someone a seat
   - Save someone's life
   - Save something to a disk
   - Save time
10. **Collocations with the verb 'Go'**
    - Go bald
    - Go abroad
    - Go bankrupt
    - Go blind
    - Go crazy
    - Go fishing
    - Go mad
    - Go missing
    - Go online
    - Go out of business
    - Go overseas
    - Go quiet
    - Go sailing
    - Go to war
11. **Collocations with the verb 'Come'**
    - Come under attack
    - Come close
    - Come direct
    - Come early
    - Come first
    - Come into view
    - Come last
    - Come late
    - Come on time
    - Come prepared
    - Come right back
    - Come to a decision
    - Come to an agreement
    - Come to an end
    - Come to a standstill
    - Come to terms with
    - Come to a total of
12. **Collocations with the verb 'Get'**
    - Get a life
    - Get a job
    - Get a shock
    - Get angry
    - Get divorced
    - Get frightened
    - Get home
    - Get lost
    - Get married
    - Get permission
    - Get ready
    - Get started
    - Get the impression

- Get upset
- Get wet
- Get worried

13. **Collocations related to 'Time'**
    - Bang on time
    - Dead on time
    - Free time
    - From dawn till dusk
    - Great deal of time
    - Make time for
    - Next few days
    - Past few weeks
    - Right on time
    - Run out of time

→ Collocation is a combination of two or more words that are often used together.

PRACTICE EXERCISE

Choose the correct option to fill in the blanks with correct collocation.

1. I am very good with hairstyles. Would you like me to _____ on your wedding day?
   (a) make your hair
   (b) set your hair
   (c) get your hair
   (d) do your hair

2. I am really hungry. Can we _____ early today?
   (a) take lunch
   (b) have lunch
   (c) lunch
   (d) lunch up

3. We worked very hard through this month. Let's _____ tonight.
   (a) have a good time
   (b) make a good time
   (c) spend a good time
   (d) good time

4. Learn all the traffic rules before you start driving. It's not good to _____.
   (a) tear the law
   (b) mess the law
   (c) break the law
   (d) hit the law

5. You _____ when you said you did not like the cake she baked.
   (a) crack her heart
   (b) broke her heart
   (c) rip her heart
   (d) kick her heart

6. Don't keep standing, _____. The discussion might take long.
   (a) seat
   (b) pull a seat
   (c) accept a seat
   (d) take a seat

7. I will really miss Judo. No one can _____ in my life.
   (a) take his place
   (b) fill his place
   (c) replace his place
   (d) share his place

8. Why do you want to give up before even _____?
   (a) making an effort
   (b) taking an effort
   (c) doing an effort
   (d) trying an effort

9. The possibility of _____ should not stop you from trying.
   (a) doing a mistake
   (b) mistake
   (c) mistaking
   (d) making a mistake

10. I did not _____ in class last week, now I don't know what to study for the test.
    (a) give attention
    (b) pay attention
    (c) offer attention
    (d) set attention

11. Sonia and Shreya promised to _____ with each other by writing letters.
    (a) in touch
    (b) put in touch
    (c) keep in touch
    (d) carry in touch

12. Switch off your computer when it is not in use. We should always _____.
    (a) use electricity
    (b) save electricity
    (c) store electricity
    (d) spend electricity

13. I am suffering from hair fall. At this rate I will _____ soon.
    (a) bald up
    (b) go bald
    (c) become bald
    (d) bald off

14. After the downpour, traffic on the road _____.
    (a) came to a standstill
    (b) became standstill
    (c) standstilled
    (d) made a standstill

15. I thought I was late, but I reached _____
    (a) correct on time
    (b) right on time
    (c) wrong on time
    (d) exact on time

16. After much deliberations and discussions, we finally _____.
    (a) came to an agreement
    (b) made an agreement
    (c) got an agreement
    (d) caught an agreement

Collocation

17. The children suffer the most when parents _____.
    (a) divorce (b) take divorce
    (c) get divorced (d) make divorce

18. We haven't made a single sale since last month. I think we will soon _____.
    (a) find out of business
    (b) go out of business
    (c) become out of business
    (d) see out of business

19. Last night, I told the taxi driver to _____ after I had paid him.
    (a) take the change
    (b) get the change
    (c) make the change
    (d) keep the change

20. I feel a bit under the weather. I think I am _____.
    (a) getting the flu (b) catching the flu
    (c) having the flu (d) flued

HOTS

Choose the right collocations from the given options.

1. I'm an ____ admirer of your work.
   (a) ardent (b) triumphant
   (c) stale (d) considerable

2. I wouldn't upset him. He can be a _____ adversary.
   (a) ardent (b) significant
   (c) unfair (d) dangerous

3. He gave me some _____ advice and I took it.
   (a) ardent (b) significant
   (c) dangerous (d) blunt

4. They don't always agree but I think there is a bond of _____ affection between them.
   (a) ugly (b) everyday
   (c) deep (d) blunt

5. It seems no time at all since I started work and here I am at _____ age.
   (a) retirement (b) old
   (c) young (d) proper

Idioms 16

Learning Objectives : In this chapter, students will learn about:
- ✓ Basic concepts of Idioms
- ✓ Some common Idioms

CHAPTER SUMMARY

An idiom is a group of words that is treated as a single unit. Idioms are also known as wise sayings. Idioms have their own specific meaning: we cannot derive the meaning of an idiom by adding the meanings of the individual words together.

The most common idioms with their meanings are following:

1. A hot potato
   Meaning: A controversial issue
2. A penny for your thoughts
   Meaning: A way of asking what someone is thinking.
3. Actions speak louder than words
   Meaning: People's intentions can be judged better by what they do than what they say.
4. Add insult to injury
   Meaning: To worsen an unfavorable situation
5. An arm and a leg
   Meaning: Very expensive or costly; a large amount of money.
6. At the drop of a hat
   Meaning: Without any hesitation; instantly.
7. Back to the drawing board
   Meaning: When an attempt fails and it's time to start from scratch.
8. Ball is in your court
   Meaning: It is up to you to make the next decision or step.
9. Barking up the wrong tree
   Meaning: Looking in the wrong place or accusing the wrong person.
10. Be glad to see the back of
    Meaning: Be happy when a person leaves
11. Beat around the bush.
    Meaning: Avoiding the main topic; not speaking directly about the issue.
12. Best of both worlds
    Meaning: Get all the advantages.
13. Best thing since sliced bread
    Meaning: A good invention or innovation.
14. Bite off more than you can chew
    Meaning: To take on a task that is beyond your capacity to complete.
15. Blessing in disguise
    Meaning: Something good that isn't recognized at first.
16. Burn the midnight oil
    Meaning: To work late into the night.
17. Can't judge a book by its cover
    Meaning: Cannot judge something based on appearance.
18. Caught between two stools
    Meaning: When someone finds it difficult to choose between two alternatives.
19. Cross that bridge when you come to it
    Meaning: Deal with a problem if and when it becomes necessary, not before.
20. Cry over spilt milk
    Meaning: When you complain about something which cannot be fixed anymore.

21. Curiosity killed the cat
    Meaning: Being inquisitive can lead you into an unpleasant situation.
22. Cut corners
    Meaning: When something is done badly to save money.
23. Devil's Advocate
    Meaning: To argue both sides
24. Don't count your chickens before the eggs have hatched.
    Meaning: Don't make plans for something that before an event.
25. Don't put all your eggs in one basket
    Meaning: Do not put all your resources in one possibility.
26. Drastic times call for drastic measures
    Meaning: When you are extremely desperate you need to take drastic actions.
27. Elvis has left the building
    Meaning: The show has come to an end.
28. Every cloud has a silver lining
    Meaning: Be optimistic, even difficult times bring something good in the end.
29. Far cry from
    Meaning: Very different from
30. Feel a bit under the weather
    Meaning: Feeling slightly ill
31. Give the benefit of the doubt
    Meaning: Believe someone's statement without proof.
32. Hear it on the grapevine
    Meaning: To hear rumours
33. Hit the nail on the head
    Meaning: Do or say something exactly right.
34. Hit the sack/hay
    Meaning: To go to bed
35. In the heat of the moment
    Meaning: Overwhelmed by what is happening in the moment.
36. It takes two to tango
    Meaning: Actions or communications that need more than one person.
37. Keep something at bay
    Meaning: Keep something away.
38. Kill two birds with one stone
    Meaning: To accomplish two different things at the same time.
39. Last straw
    Meaning: The final problem in a series of problems.
40. Let sleeping dogs lie
    Meaning: Leave a situation as it is.
41. Let the cat out of the bag
    Meaning: To share information that was previously hidden.

TRIVIA

The word 'Goodbye' originally comes from an Old English phrase meaning 'God be with you'.

42. Make a long story short
    Meaning: Come to the point; leave out details.
43. Miss the boat
    Meaning: Someone has missed his or her chance.
44. Not a spark of decency
    Meaning: No manners
45. Not playing with a full deck
    Meaning: Someone who lacks intelligence.
46. On the ball
    Meaning: When someone understands the situation well.
47. Once in a blue moon
    Meaning: Happens very rarely
48. Picture paints a thousand words
    Meaning: A visual presentation is far more descriptive than words.
49. Piece of cake
    Meaning: A job, task or other activity that is easy or simple.
50. See eye to eye
    Meaning: When two (or more people) agree on something.
51. Sit on the fence
    Meaning: When someone does not want to choose or make a decision.
52. Speak of the devil!
    Meaning: When the person you have just been talking about arrives.

53. Steal someone's thunder
    Meaning: To take the credit for something someone else did.
54. Take with a grain of salt
    Meaning: Not to take what someone says too seriously.
55. Taste of your own medicine
    Meaning: Something happens to you, or is done to you, that you have done to someone else.
56. To hear something straight from the horse's mouth
    Meaning: To hear something from the authoritative source.
57. Whole nine yards
    Meaning: Everything
58. Wouldn't be caught dead
    Meaning: Would never like to do something.
59. Your guess is as good as mine
    Meaning: To have no idea, do not know the answer to a question.

MUST REMEMBER

➡ An idiom is a group of words that is treated as a single unit. Idioms are also known as wise sayings. Idioms have their own specific meaning.

PRACTICE EXERCISE

I. Choose the correct option/idiom to fill in the blanks.

1. He always tells his parents that he loves them, but he never actually does anything nice for them. Someone should teach him that _____.
   (a) actions speak louder than words
   (b) blessing in disguise
   (c) curiosity killed the cat
   (d) burn the midnight oil

2. Our boss expects us to show up in her office _____, even when we're in a meeting with clients.
   (a) caught between two stools
   (b) at the drop of a hat
   (c) cry over spilt milk
   (d) far cry from

3. Come to the point directly, there is no use _____.
   (a) every cloud has a silver lining
   (b) kill two birds with one stone
   (c) beating around the bush
   (d) last straw

4. We could not reach the restaurant as it was raining heavily. Everyone who ate there that night got food poisoning. I guess the bad weather was _____.
   (a) blessing in disguise
   (b) keep something at bay
   (c) it takes two to tango
   (d) once in a blue moon

5. She was mad that he broke her vase. But there's no use _____, so she forgave him.
   (a) not a spark of decency
   (b) miss the boat
   (c) Elvis has left the building
   (d) crying over spilt milk

6. Last night, my math homework was a _____. I finished it in ten minutes.
   (a) hit the nail on the head
   (b) piece of cake
   (c) sit on the fence
   (d) on the ball

7. She works in the city and lives in the country. So, she gets _____.
   (a) see eye to eye
   (b) whole nine yards
   (c) best of both worlds
   (d) not a spark of decency

8. Sally blames Tracy for the fight. Well it can't be Tracy alone. _____.
   (a) Take with a grain of salt
   (b) It takes two to tango
   (c) Speak of the Devil!
   (d) Taste of your own medicine

9. A total solar eclipse is a rare phenomenon. It happens _____.
   (a) your guess is as good as mine
   (b) let the sleeping dogs lie
   (c) once in a blue moon
   (d) in the heat of the moment

10. My dad hates going to parties. He _____ in one.
    (a) hit the sack
    (b) cross that bridge when you come to it
    (c) caught between two stools
    (d) wouldn't be caught dead

11. I was going to announce my wedding dates. But she _____ by announcing it before me.
    (a) stole my thunder
    (b) cut corners
    (c) bite off more than you can chew
    (d) beat around the bush

12. I'm sorry your business is not doing well at the moment. But don't worry, _____.
    (a) every cloud has a silver lining
    (b) be glad to see the back of
    (c) actions speak louder than words
    (d) add insult to injury

13. I won't _____ just to save money. For me, quality comes first.
    (a) an arm and a leg
    (b) cut corners
    (c) barking up the wrong tree
    (d) add insult to injury

14. I have _____ to make this show happen. I will take the credit for it.
    (a) blessing in disguise
    (b) best of both worlds
    (c) burned the midnight oil
    (d) cut corners
15. Jake always avoided pineapple because he did not like its hard and spiky exterior. But a friend of his cut a slice for him to eat the other day and Jake seemed to like it. You should never _____.
    (a) cry over spilt milk
    (b) curiosity killed the cat
    (c) feel a bit under the weather
    (d) judge a book by its cover

II. **Choose the correct option that matches the given idiom.**
1. Elvis has left the building
    (a) very different from
    (b) the show has come to an end
    (c) to hear rumours
    (d) do or say something exactly right
2. Kill two birds with one stone
    (a) to accomplish two different things at the same time
    (b) someone has missed his or her chance
    (c) no manners
    (d) happens very rarely
3. Sit on the fence
    (a) to take the credit for something some-one else did.
    (b) when two (or more people) agree on something.
    (c) when someone does not want to choose or make a decision.
    (d) not to take what someone says too seriously.
4. Whole nine yards
    (a) would never like to do something
    (b) to hear something from the authoritative source.
    (c) a job, task or other activity that is easy or simple.
    (d) everything
5. Speak of the devil!
    (a) when the person you have just been talking about arrives.
    (b) when someone understands the situation well.
    (c) happens very rarely
    (d) leave a situation as it is
6. Make a long story short
    (a) to share information that was previously hidden.
    (b) come to the point; leave out details.
    (c) to take the credit for something someone else did.
    (d) very different from
7. Don't put all your eggs in one basket
    (a) when something is done badly to save money.
    (b) don't make plans for something that might not happen.
    (c) do not put all your resources in one possibility.
    (d) be optimistic, even difficult times bring something good in the end.
8. Curiosity killed the cat
    (a) when something is done badly to save money.
    (b) when you complain about something which cannot be fixed anymore.
    (c) when someone finds it difficult to choose between two alternatives.
    (d) being inquisitive can lead you into an unpleasant situation.
9. Best thing since sliced bread
    (a) get all the advantages
    (b) a good invention or innovation
    (c) something good that isn't recognized at first.
    (d) when an attempt fails and it's time to start from scratch
10. Be glad to see the back of
    (a) when an attempt fails and it's time to start from scratch.
    (b) looking in the wrong place or accusing the wrong person.
    (c) be happy when a person leaves
    (d) avoiding the main topic; not speaking directly about the issue.

HOTS

Some proverbs/idioms are given below together with their meanings. Choose the correct meaning of proverb/idiom, If there is no correct meaning given, E (i.e.) 'None of these' will be the answer.

1. To make clean breast of
   (a) To gain prominence
   (b) To praise oneself
   (c) To confess without of reserve
   (d) To destroy before it blooms
   (e) None of these
2. To keeps one's temper
   (a) To become hungry
   (b) To be in good mood
   (c) To preserve ones energy
   (d) To be aloof from
   (e) None of these
3. To catch a tartar
   (a) To trap wanted criminal with great difficulty
   (b) To catch a dangerous person
   (c) To meet with disaster
   (d) To deal with a person who is more than one's match
   (e) None of these
4. To drive home
   (a) To find one's roots
   (b) To return to place of rest
   (c) Back to original position
   (d) To emphasise
   (e) None of these
5. To have an axe to grind
   (a) A private end to serve
   (b) To fail to arouse interest
   (c) To have no result
   (d) To work for both sides
   (e) None of these

Vocabulary   17

Learning Objectives : In this chapter, students will learn about:
- ✓ Basic concepts of Vocabulary – some everyday problems, relationships, travel and health related

CHAPTER SUMMARY

Words help us express our thoughts. Let us take a look at some word groups related to a common man's daily life.

Everyday problems
Miss a flight, Stuck in traffic, Late for dinner, Late for work/school, Lack of sleep, Water scarcity, Crowded public transport, Overworked, Competition, Bad weather, Animal cruelty, Pollution, Price rise, Power cut, Waterlogging, Corruption

Relationships
Father, Mother, Husband, Wife, Son, Daughter, Brother, Sister, Grandparents, Grandchildren, Aunt, Uncle, Nephew, Niece, Son-in law, Daughter-in-law, Parents, Twin, Friend, Married, Divorced, Engaged, Single

Travel
Airport, Check-in, Fly, Land, Take off, Passport, Ticket, Journey, Passenger, Route, Travel agent, Trip, Luggage, Sightseeing, Tourist, Suitcase, Train, Railway station, Road, Board,

 **TRIVIA**

Any number with a series of repeating digits, like 7777, is called "Repdigit"

Health
Headache, Stomach ache, Toothache, Cancer, Cold, Cough, Flu, Heart attack, Infection, Pain, Virus, Bruise, Cut, Wound, Bandage, Check-up, Dose (of medicine), Drugs, Injection, Medicine, Operation, Pill, Plaster, Dentist, Doctor, Nurse, Patient, Surgeon, Hospital, Operating Theatre, Surgery, Prescription, Treatment, Fit, Ill, Sick, Healthy, Unwell, Well, Pharmacy

- ➤ A vocabulary is a set of familiar words within a person's language.
- ➤ A vocabulary, usually developed with age, serves as a useful and fundamental tool for communication and acquiring knowledge.

PRACTICE EXERCISE

I. Everyday Problems

Fill in the blanks with the correct option.

1. It is really upsetting when your _____ because of no fault of yours. It was due to bad traffic.
   (a) miss a flight
   (b) catch a flight
   (c) flight delayed
   (d) reach on time

2. I have sat in office till late every day this week. I feel _____.
   (a) rested   (b) overslept
   (c) overworked   (d) relaxed

3. In the corporate world, a little bit of healthy _____ often helps us achieve greater things. But we should stop before it becomes rivalry.
   (a) pollution   (b) competition
   (c) traffic   (d) weather

4. _____ is the urban menace that affects the poor of the society most.
   (a) price rise   (b) excessive heat
   (c) traffic   (d) rainfall

5. I love animals. I would like to work with an organization that fights _____.
   (a) power cut   (b) waterlogging
   (c) competition   (d) animal cruelty

II. Relationships

Fill in the blanks with the correct option.

1. My sister has to travel abroad for work. She wants me look after her two-year-old daughter in her absence. I will be picking up my _____ on my way home from work today.
   (a) niece   (b) nephew
   (c) sister   (d) cousin

2. Mr and Mrs Reynolds have been like second _____ to Carrie since she was a child.
   (a) friend   (b) daughter
   (c) son   (d) parents

3. From the time Mahesh has married Pooja, he has been looking after her parents like his own. He is an ideal _____.
   (a) son   (b) son-in-law
   (c) nephew   (d) grandson

4. The best people to tell you about your parent's childhood are your _____.
   (a) grandchildren   (b) son
   (c) grandparents   (d) daughter

5. A female sibling is a _____ and a male sibling is a _____.
   (a) sister/brother (b) aunt/uncle
   (c) niece/nephew   (d) wife/husband

III. Travel

Fill in the blanks with the correct option.

1. The _____ counter at the airport is where we are supposed to leave our baggage.
   (a) check-in   (b) take-off
   (c) check-out   (d) check-off

2. My house is close to the _____. You can always hear one train or the other chugging past.
   (a) airport   (b) bus stand
   (c) railway station (d) port

3. We start out five-day road trip tomorrow. We must decide which _____ to take before we head out.
   (a) journey   (b) route
   (c) land   (d) trip

4. Have you ever travelled without a _____? I would be scared of getting caught by a ticket-checker.
   (a) suitcase   (b) boarding pass
   (c) passport   (d) ticket

5. You cannot travel abroad without a valid _____.
   (a) passport   (b) luggage
   (c) travel agent   (d) passenger

IV. Health

Fill in the blanks with the correct option.

1. If you have a _____ you must visit the dentist.
   (a) headache   (b) toothache
   (c) stomach ache   (d) heart attack

2. Under a microscope, some _____ appear very beautiful.
   (a) viruses   (b) wounds
   (c) drugs   (d) pill
3. Brent fractured his arm and had to wear a _____ for three weeks.
   (a) pill   (b) operation
   (c) plaster   (d) dose
4. Doctors conduct surgery in the _____. Outside the door of the room, a red light is left on until the procedure is complete.
   (a) operation theatre
   (b) hospital
   (c) pharmacy
   (d) cafeteria
5. If you are feeling _____, you must not go to work. Germs can spread easily.
   (a) well   (b) fit
   (c) healthy   (d) ill

HOTS

I. **Fill in the blanks with correct option.**
1. It's time to get rid of the old team and _____ in some fresh ideas.
   (a) set   (b) be
   (c) come   (d) bring
2. I'm very unhappy with the service and I intend to _____ in a complaint.
   (a) cave   (b) take
   (c) dig   (d) put
3. I don't feel we can cope with this and I suggest we _____ in Judith to help us with this.
   (a) come   (b) give
   (c) bring   (d) be
4. The company was in serious financial trouble, so they decided to _____ in the receivers.
   (a) dig   (b) take
   (c) call   (d) be
5. It seems a shame to call off the project after all the hard work you have _____ in.
   (a) put   (b) give
   (c) cave   (d) dig

II. **Read the following information and choose the best option.**
1. When you get angry, you usually
   (a) throw things
   (b) withdraw yourself and start crying
   (c) leave the situation and engage yourself in a different activity.
   (d) None of these
2. While attending your friend's party, you see your friend's muffler catching fire from the candle on the table behind him. You would
   (a) ask your friend to see behind him
   (b) rush to friend's mother
   (c) rush and taking out the muffler from his neck, drop it and pour water on it.
   (d) take out the muffler and through it away
3. While travelling in a train, you notice a man from the coach behind yours fall off the train. You would
   (a) pull the alarm chain so that the train may stop and the man may be helped.
   (b) shout at the falling man asking him to get up quickly and entrain.
   (c) jump off the trian to assist the falling man.
   (d) wait till the train stops a the next station and inform the railway authorities there.
4. When you see a blind man trying to cross the road, you
   (a) ask someone to help him
   (b) go and help him
   (c) wait till he crosses the road
   (d) ignore and move on
5. You have gone to enjoy a Diwali Mela organized by a club. Suddenly you come across a lost child crying desperately. You would
   (a) neglect and walk away
   (b) ask the child to find his parents
   (c) ask him to stop crying and wait patiently for his parents.
   (d) contact with the club authorities and make an announcement for the parents.

Vocabulary

SECTION 2
READING COMPREHENSION

Reading Comprehension

News Headlines
Newspaper is the source of information mainly on current news, happenings, current affairs, and various other events around the word.

Newspaper
A newspaper is a daily publication containing news, other informative articles, and usually advertising. The paper is usually printed on relatively inexpensive, low-grade paper known as newsprint. Most newspapers now publish online as well as in print. The online versions are called online newspapers or news sites.

Newspapers are typically published daily or weekly. News magazines are also weekly, but they have a magazine format. General-interest newspapers typically publish news articles and feature articles on national and international news as well as local news. The news includes political events and personalities, business and finance, crime, severe weather, and natural disasters; health and medicine, science, and technology; sports; and entertainment, society, food and cooking, clothing and home fashion, and the arts. Typically the paper is divided into sections for each of those major groupings. Most traditional papers also feature an editorial page containing editorials written by an editor, op-eds written by guest writers, and columns that express the personal opinions of columnists, usually offering analysis and synthesis that attempts to translate the raw data of the news into information telling the reader "what it all means" and persuading them to concur.

A wide variety of material has been published in newspapers. Besides the aforementioned news and opinions, they include weather forecasts; criticism and reviews of the arts (including literature, film, television, theatre, fine arts, and architecture) and of local services such as restaurants; obituaries; entertainment features such as crosswords, horoscopes, editorial cartoons, gag cartoons, and comic strips; advice, food, and other columns; and radio and television listings (program schedules).

Most newspapers are businesses, and they pay their expenses (such as journalists' wages, printing costs, and distribution costs) with a mixture of subscription revenue, newsstand sales, and advertising revenue (other businesses or individuals pay to place advertisements in the pages, including display ads, classified ads, and their online equivalents). Some newspapers are government-run or at least government-funded; their reliance on advertising revenue and on profitability is less critical to their survival. The editorial independence of a newspaper is thus always subject to the interests of someone, whether owners, advertisers, or a government. Some newspapers with high editorial independence, high journalism quality, and large circulation are viewed as newspapers of record.

Brochure
A brochure is an informative paper document (often also used for advertising), that can be folded into a template, pamphlet or leaflet. Brochures are advertising pieces mainly used to introduce a company or organization and inform about products and/or services to a target audience.

Brochures are distributed by radio, handed out personally or placed in brochure racks. They may be considered as grey literature. They are usually present near tourist attractions.

Kinds of Brochures
Brochures are now available in electronic format and are called e-brochures. The most common types of single-sheet brochures are the bi-fold (a single sheet printed on both sides and folded into halves) and the tri-fold (the same, but folded into thirds). A bi-fold brochure results in four panels (two panels on each side), while a tri-fold results in six panels (three panels on each side).

Other brochure fold arrangements are possible: "z-fold" method, the "c-fold" method, etc. Larger sheets, such as those with detailed maps or expansive photo spreads, are folded into four, five, or six panels. When two card fascia are affixed to the outer panels of the z-folded brochure, it is commonly known as a "z-card".

Booklet brochures are made of multiple sheets most often saddle-stitched, stapled on the creased edge, or perfect bound like a paperback book, and result in eight or more panels.

Brochures are often printed using four-color process on thick, glossy paper to give an initial impression of quality. Businesses may print small quantities of brochures on a computer printer or on a digital printer, but offset printing turns out higher quantities for less cost.

Compared with a flyer, a brochure usually uses higher-quality paper, more colour, and is folded.

A letter is the means of communication between two persons, direct or personal, written or printed message addressed to a person or organization.

Types of Letters

Formal Letters

Formal letters are sent to organization, government departments, etc. to make complaints, request, inquiries, orders etc. In case of formal letters, the person to whom you are addressing the letter is not a friend or any other person known to you. Your tone should be respect making use of formal words and sentences to create a nice impression on the recipient. Formal letters follow a set format where you write the name, designation, and address of the recipient, full on the top left while your own name and address at the top right. You sign off at the bottom left under yours truly or yours faithfully.

Specimen Formal Letter

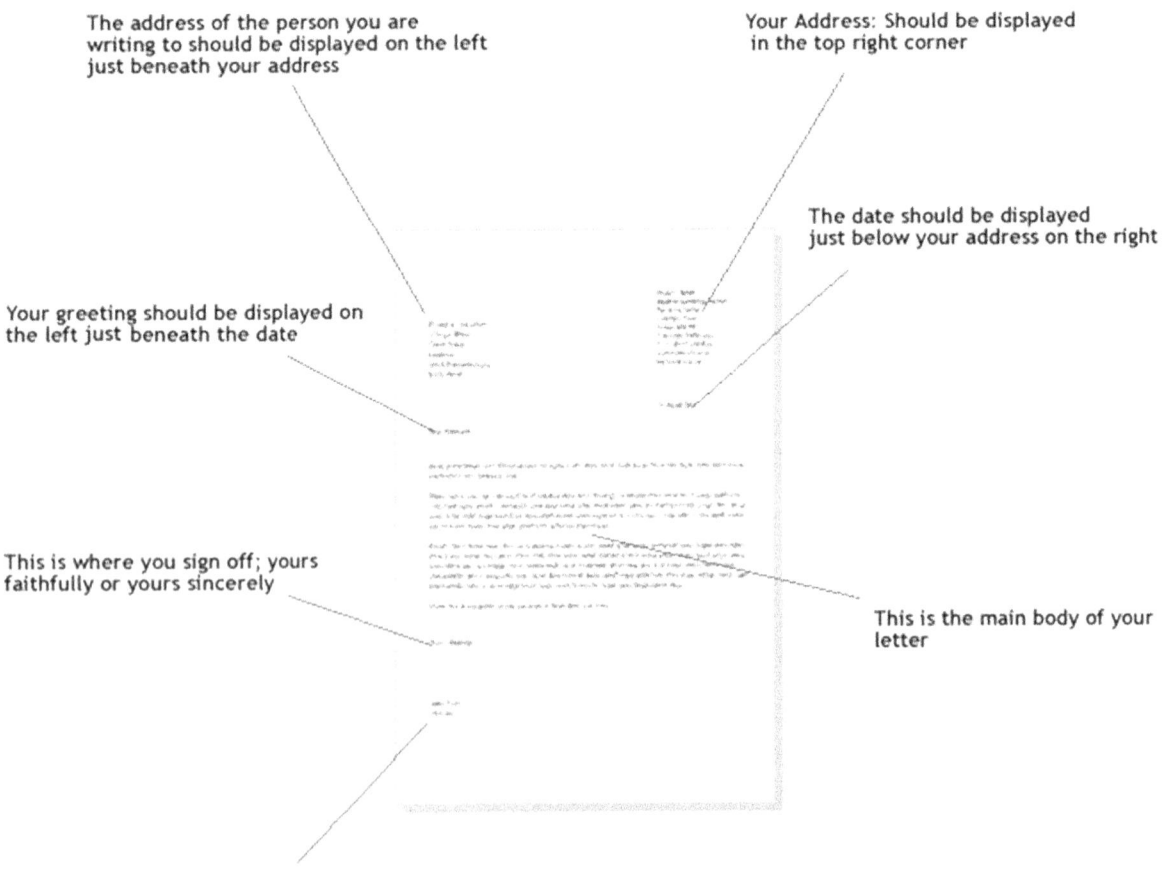

Informal Letters

Informal letters are written to friends, parents, relatives and acquaintances. The purpose of writing a letter is not to make a complaint or inquiry, and the tone is also casual. The words used can be colloquial and slang, and you are not there to create an impression. Informal letters can be considered a freestyle swimming where you are free to write in the style and tone as you wish. There is no set format, and there is no need to use formal style and tone.

Specimen Informal Letter

Address of Writer/Sender
Date
Greeting (informal)

Body of the letter

With love/ Best wishes
(Your name)
(and signature)

PRACTICE EXERCISE

I. **Read the following newspaper headlines and choose the correct option to answer the questions that follow.**

THE NEWARK ADVOCATE — 12 Pages

WORST OCEAN DISASTER IN WORLD'S HISTORY; TITANIC GOES DOWN; 1,341 LIVES ARE LOST

STEAMER CARPATHIA HAS 868 SURVIVORS OF ILL-FATED BOAT

ENTIRE WORLD STUNNED BY NEWS OF DISASTER TO THE STEAMER TITANIC

1. What is the name of the newspaper in which the article has been published?
   (a) The New York Times
   (b) The Daily Mirror
   (c) The Newark Advocate
   (d) London Herald
2. How many people are killed?
   (a) 868   (b) 1,341
   (c) 2,200   (d) 1,500
3. Some of the survivors were rescued by…
   (a) Carpathia
   (b) The government
   (c) Sailors
   (d) Family members
4. How many pages does the newspaper have?
   (a) 12   (b) 5
   (c) 24   (d) 17
5. Whose family were Titanic passengers?
   (a) Captain of Carpathia
   (b) Someone who works with the newspaper
   (c) A famous actor
   (d) A politician

II. **Read the newspaper headlines given below and choose the correct option to complete the report.**

1. A Delhi girl wins 4 medals at Special Olympics.
(i) A _____ has won four medals at the Special Olympics.
   (a) girl from Delhi
   (b) girl who came to visit Delhi
   (c) girl called Delhi
   (d) girl participating in a competition held in Delhi
(ii) Special Olympics is a _____ held for differently-abled people.
   (a) talent hunt   (b) sports event
   (c) music festival   (d) drama contest
2. Rain plays havoc, brings city to standstill.
(i) Weekend revelers and shoppers were caught unaware with a _____ on Sunday evening.
   (a) sudden shower
   (b) procession
   (c) a street football match
   (d) road block
(ii) The rain lashed most parts of the city, leading to _____.
   (a) potholes
   (b) people getting drenched
   (c) massive traffic jam
   (d) a procession of umbrellas
3. Mysore Zoo welcomes new guest.
(i) A _____ was born in Mysore Zoo on Saturday.
   (a) a girl child
   (b) female giraffe
   (c) a boy child
   (d) a pair of twins
(ii) Five-year-old Khushi and her male companion Krishnaraja have named the _____ Radha.
   (a) daughter   (b) son
   (c) child   (d) calf

III. **Read the brochure and choose the correct option to answer the questions that follow.**

LANGUAGE CENTRE

presents

Talkwell,

a Holiday Camp for Children

Ever paid attention to your child's spoken English? Have you wondered how to improve his or her vocabulary?

Considering how important it is to speak English fluently and with confidence in this competitive world, it is natural for you to worry about your child's command over the English language.

LANGUAGE CENTRE in collaboration with ELLI, the English Language Learning Institute USA presents Talkwell, a fun-filled holiday camp for primary children where they will learn to speak English correctly and fluently.

Taught through interactive games and activities, the training ensures that children learn and practice what they have learnt.

Online applications are welcome. Email: www.langcentre.com

Or or step into any of our centres.

Duration of course: 4 weeks

Last date of application: One week before the beginning of June holidays

Free Early Bird Prizes

1. The camp advertised is to help children to be able to
   (a) read and write English
   (b) speak English correctly and fluently
   (c) score top marks
   (d) impress others
2. The name of the course is
   (a) Talksmart   (b) Talkwell
   (c) Language Centre (d) ELLI
3. What is the duration of the course?
   (a) 3 weeks   (b) 4 days
   (c) 4 weeks   (d) 4 months
4. The encourage enrolment, the advertiser offers
   (a) computer-based programmes
   (b) free prizes
   (c) discounts
   (d) free registration
5. What is the full form of ELLI?
   (a) English Language and Literature Institute
   (b) English Learning Language Institute
   (c) English Language Learning Institute
   (d) English Learning Leading Institute

IV. **Read the brochure and choose the correct option to answer the questions that follow.**

FREEDOM CARNIVAL
HELIOS THE WATCH STORE
WISHES YOU A HAPPY INDEPENDENCE DAY & INVITES YOU TO
HELIOS END OF SEASON
SALE
UPTO 50 % OFF
ON OVER 25 INTERNATIONAL BRANDS
+
Additional 5% OFF
For first 50 customers
From 13th to 16th August, 2015 at Helios – The Watch Store

Esplanade Crossing: 2nd Block, Park Square Road
Nehru Nagar: 100 Feet Road, Mall Junction
Rajabazar: 3/6 Oberoi Building, Near Music World

1. Why is the company having a sale?
   (a) to celebrate Diwali
   (b) to celebrate Independence Day
   (c) it's the annual sale
   (d) to clear stock
2. Who is going to get an additional 5% off?
   (a) company staff
   (b) previous owners of Helios watches
   (c) first 50 customers
   (d) those who have membership cards
3. What is the name of the sale?
   (a) Freedom Carnival
   (b) Freedom Fest
   (c) Freedom Sale
   (d) Freedom Celebrations
4. For how many days will the sale be on?
   (a) 10 days
   (b) 2 weeks
   (c) whole of August
   (d) 4 days
5. How much discount has been announced?
   (a) 50 %   (b) Up to 50 %
   (c) 25 %   (d) 15 %

V. Read the itinerary and choose the correct option to answer the questions that follow.

Three Days in Mumbai

Day 1: Kolkata to Mumbai

Travel from Kolkata airport on an Air India flight to Mumbai. On arrival in Mumbai our friendly local representatives will be there to greet you and transfer you to your hotel. Enjoy the rest of the day relaxing.

Day 2: Mumbai Sightseeing

This morning, enjoy the sights of Mumbai on a city tour. Start your Mumbai *darshan* with the Gateway of India – Mumbai's famous monument and the best starting point for tourist to explore the city. Take a drive up the Malabar Hill to the lovely Hanging Gardens and the Kamla Nehru Park. Then experience the wonderful view of Mumbai and the Arabian Sea.

Day 3: Mumbai Markets and Munchies

Mumbai locals love to shop and eat, and with some of the best markets in the country to browse, there's no reason why you shouldn't join in. Whether you're looking for jewellery, saris, antiques or contemporary fashion, you'll find it at one of Mumbai's many markets. When you're feeling hungry after all the hard bargaining, head to Chowpatty Beach at dusk to watch the sunset and snack on Mumbai street food.

Day 4: Harbor and Caves Excursion

What better way to spend your last day in Mumbai than by admiring the port before taking a scenic boat cruise over the waters of Mumbai Harbour. Or ride a ferry over to Elephanta Island, to explore the caverns and the beautiful Hindu temple sculptures of the Elephanta Caves.

1. Which airline are the tourists going to fly through?
   (a) Air India
   (b) Indian Airlines
   (c) Indigo
   (d) Spice Jet

2. What will the tourists see on Day 1?
   (a) the beach
   (b) The Gateway of India
   (c) the harbor
   (d) none of the above

3. Which water body are we close to when we are in Mumbai?
   (a) Indian Ocean
   (b) Bay of Bengal
   (c) Arabian Sea
   (d) Andaman Sea

4. What do the tourists do on Day 3?
   (a) sightseeing
   (b) cruise
   (c) eat and shop
   (d) return home

5. How will the tourists reach the Elephanta Island?
   (a) car
   (b) ferry
   (c) walk down
   (d) bus

VI. Read the letter given below and choose the correct option to answer the questions that follow.

G135, 2nd Floor,
Vasant Kunj Apartments
New Delhi 110019

Lifestyle Stores
Vasant Kunj Mall
New Delhi

Dear Sir/Madam,

On March 5, 2010, I bought a Tolke-in Idli Kit from your store at the Vasant Kunj Mall. The cashier who assisted me was Rajesh. He was very friendly and assured me that the Tolke-in Idli Kit would live up to the guarantee on the box and produce perfect idlis each time.

Unfortunately, this product did not live up to its claim. The idlis I made were far from perfect. I followed the directions included in the package very carefully. First, I removed the bag of mix from the box. Then, I poured it into a bowl. Next, I added the correct amount of water to the mix and stirred it. Finally, I poured the mix into the idli tins and kept it in the oven at 350 degrees for exactly 20 minutes.

When the idlis finished cooking, I was very excited to eat them. You can imagine my disappointment when, upon tasting the idlis, I discovered that they were not perfect. These idlis were, in fact, absolutely terrible.

I would appreciate a full refund (Rs 1,500) for this product as soon as possible. Enclosed are the receipt, the empty box, and one of the un-perfect idlis so that you can experience it for yourself. Thank you for your prompt attention to this matter.

Sincerely,
Manoj Saxena

1. This letter is most likely addressed to
   (a) the owner of the idli kit company
   (b) local storeowner
   (c) the clerk at a local idli joint
   (d) Rajesh, the cashier who sold the idli kit
2. The tone of the author can best be described as
   (a) furious
   (b) disgusted
   (c) embarrassed
   (d) frustrated
3. As used in paragraph 1, which is the best synonym for guarantee?
   (a) lie
   (b) warning
   (c) promise
   (d) sentence
4. The author is disappointed by the product because
   (a) it was worth less money than he paid for it
   (b) it did not fulfill the promise made on the box
   (c) the directions included with the product contained a mistake
   (d) the directions included with the product were too difficult to follow
5. The author's main purpose in writing this letter is to
   (a) complain about how bad the idlis tasted
   (b) obtain a full refund for his money
   (c) prevent others from making the same mistake he did
   (d) persuade the company to change the wording on their box

VII. Read the letter given below and choose the correct option to answer the questions that follow

Shruti Singh (Class 6th),
Daffodils Primary School
New Delhi

Mr Shankar,
Best Foods
New Delhi

Dear Sir,

This year, we, the students of Class 6, at the Daffodils Primary School are focusing on the environment and recycling as one of our projects. We are learning as much as possible about environmental issues and how we can help by "being green".

Our teacher told us that you have spare cardboard boxes at your company's warehouse, and we are hoping you will be willing to donate these to our school for use in our compost bins and wormfarm. We are also working on a whole-school art project in which we create the entire contents of a classroom from recycled materials. This includes chairs, tables, shelves, a teacher's desk and even a computer! We are enjoying it very much. Some students have even been volunteering to work on the project during lunch times. Once the room is finished, we will have an exhibition for parents and other members to come and see the recycled classroom and all our other green initiatives, and we promise to invite you. We hope that our community will be inspired to think about how they can do more for the environment.

We would very much like you to be involved and hope that you will agree to contribute.

Yours sincerely,
Shruti Singh (Class 6, Daffodils Primary School)

1. This letter has been written by
   (a) a student of class 6
   (b) a teacher
   (c) a parent
   (d) an environment activist
2. This year the concerned class is focusing on
   (a) computers and technology
   (b) cooking and baking
   (c) environment and recycling
   (d) art and craft
3. Why has the letter been written?
   (a) to ask for spare cardboard boxes
   (b) to invite people to the exhibition
   (c) to promote awareness about the environment
   (d) to announce sale of recycled products
4. The students are making a classroom with
   (a) wood
   (b) paper
   (c) recycled materials
   (d) plastic

5. What does the class promise Mr Shankar?
   (a) to return the cardboard boxes
   (b) to gift him some the products they make
   (c) to pay him a visit
   (d) to invite him to the school exhibition

VIII. Read the letter given below and choose the correct option to answer the questions that follow.

18.05.2023

Dear Kavita,

Hi! I am sorry it took me so long to write. I have been really busy with school and setting up the new apartment.

How are things with you? When does your school reopen? I wish the summer vacations end soon. The only reason I say this is because I want school to start and finish quickly. This is the last year in school and I want to start going to college as soon as possible.

I miss you! I loved being in Mumbai and I am so sad to have to come back to Delhi.

I loved all the friends I made there, especially you.

How is the preparation for the annual school fest going? What are the events our school is partici-pating in? We always shine in the singing and dancing rounds. I wish I was there now.

I hope all is well with you. Give your family my love. I don't have my pictures back yet but I will soon, so I will mail you some then.

Write back soon.

Love,

Archana

1. What is the relationship between Kavita and Archana?
   (a) sisters
   (b) mother and daughter
   (c) friends
   (d) cousins

2. Kavita had to move from
   (a) Mumbai to Delhi
   (b) Delhi to Mumbai
   (c) Mumbai to Kolkata
   (d) None of the above

3. Archana wants summer vacation to end because
   (a) she wants to get back to school
   (b) she hates summer
   (c) she has lot of holiday homework
   (d) she is feeling bored

4. What does Archana say she will mail back later?
   (a) pictures
   (b) address
   (c) phone number
   (d) some important information

5. Which class do you think Archana is in?
   (a) Class 9
   (b) Class 6
   (c) Class 7
   (d) Class 12

IX. Read the letter given below and choose the correct option to answer the questions that follow.

23rd November

Dear Adil,

I'm going away for five days to visit Grandma. She's not feeling well. I am sorry that I could not meet you before leaving.

Be a good boy. Get ready early so that you don't miss the school bus and reach school on time. Don't forget your piano lesson after school this afternoon.

Aunt Sheila will be there when you get back from school for these few days. I have explained to her what you like to eat and what not. She will prepare lunch and dinner for you. Ask for her help if you need anything. Remember to be polite.

Do your homework before dinner. Remember, no TV after 9 p.m.!

This Saturday is your dad's birthday. Please make a nice card for him. I will ask Aunt Sheila to order a cake for him. You can call me at 7708134751.

Love,

Mom

1. What does Adil do after school today?
   (a) Attend a piano lesson
   (b) Play football with his friends
   (c) Finish his homework
   (d) Visit his grandmother
2. What are the two behaviour related things Adil's Mom asks him to do?
   (a) Be gentle and soft-spoken
   (b) Be disciplined
   (c) Be good and polite
   (d) Be obedient
3. Whose birthday is it on Saturday?
   (a) Adil's Mom
   (b) Adil's Grandmother
   (c) Adil's Father
   (d) Aunt Sheila's
4. What can't Adil do after 9 pm?
   (a) Sleep   (b) Have dinner
   (c) Play the piano   (d) Watch TV
5. When is Adil's Mom returning?
   (a) 24 November   (b) 24 December
   (c) 28 November   (d) 28 December

X. Read the passage and answer the questions that follow.

There was once a king of Scotland whose name was Robert Bruce. He needed to be both brave and wise because the times in which he lived were wild and rude. The King of England was at war with him and had led a great army into Scotland to drive him out of the land.

Battle after battle had been fought. Six times Bruce had led his brave little army against his foes and six times his men had been beaten and driven into flight. At last his army was scattered, and he was forced to hide himself in the woods and in lonely places among the mountains.

One rainy day, Bruce lay on the ground under a rude shed listening to the patter of the drops on the roof above him. He was tired and sick at heart and ready to give up all hope. It seemed to him that there was no use for him to try to do anything more.

As he lay thinking, he saw a spider over his head making ready to weave her web. He watched her as she toiled slowly and with great care. Six times she tried to throw her frail thread from one beam to another, and six times it fell short.

"Poor thing," said Bruce: "you, too, know what it is to fail."

But the spider did not lose hope with the sixth failure. With still more care, she made ready to try for the seventh time. Bruce almost forgot his own troubles as he watched her swing herself out upon the slender line. Would she fail again? No! The thread was carried safely to the beam and fastened there.

"I, too, will try a seventh time!" cried Bruce.

He arose and called his men together. He told them of his plans and sent them out with messages of cheer to his disheartened people. Soon there was an army of brave Scotchmen around him. Another battle was fought, and the King of England was glad to go back into his own country.

1. Robert Bruce was the king of which country?
   (a) England   (b) Scotland
   (c) Netherland   (d) Ireland
2. What is the meaning of the word 'foe' as used in second paragraph?
   (a) countrymen   (b) army
   (c) enemies   (d) family members
3. What was the weather like on the day Bruce spotted the spider?
   (a) it was raining
   (b) it was bright and sunny
   (c) it was cold and grey
   (d) it was windy
4. In how many attempts did the spider succeed to make its web?
   (a) six
   (b) one
   (c) seven
   (d) it did not succeed
5. What lesson does Bruce learn from the spider?
   (a) there is hope in the end
   (b) we cannot win always
   (c) slow and steady win the race
   (d) try, try again until you succeed

XI. **Read the passage and answer the questions that follow.**

Mount Rushmore known as "The Presidents' Mountain" is located in the Black Hills of South Dakota. Doane Robinson thought of the idea to have a stoned carved monument as one way to attract people from all over the country to come to his state. Robinson met with Gutzon Borglum, the sculptor who worked on Stone Mountain in Georgia. Borglum selected the location for Mount Rushmore and Robinson worked to get funding for this project.

The faces of four American Presidents are carved on this mountain. The four presidents carved in the mountain are George Washington, Thomas Jefferson, Theodore Roosevelt and Abraham Lincoln. Gutzon Borglum chose these four presidents because he felt they represented the first 150 years of American history.

Washington as first president represents the birth of the country. Jefferson stands for the expansion of the nation as he is credited with the Louisiana Purchase in 1803. Lincoln symbolizes the preservation of the nation in leading the nation through the challenging Civil War. Theodore Roosevelt represents the development of the country.

It took 14 years to complete Mount Rushmore. Nearly 400 workers helped create this memorial.

1. What is another name for Mount Rushmore?
   (a) The American Mountain
   (b) The Four Men's Mountain
   (c) The Presidents' Mountain
   (d) The Great Rushmore
2. Which two persons designed and built this monument?
   (a) Thomas Jefferson
   (b) Doane Robinson and Gutzon Borglum
   (c) Theodore Roosevelt
   (d) Abraham Lincoln
3. What does Mount Rushmore symbolize?
   (a) a stone carving
   (b) a tourist attraction
   (c) four great American Presidents
   (d) an ecosystem
4. Who was the first president of America?
   (a) George Washington
   (b) Thomas Jefferson
   (c) Theodore Roosevelt
   (d) Abraham Lincoln
5. Which of these is NOT true about Mount Rushmore?
   (a) it took 14 years to build it
   (b) about 400 workers helped construct it
   (c) it is located in Georgia
   (d) Borglum selected the location for it

XII. **Read the poem and answer the questions that follow.**

I know a funny little man,
As quiet as a mouse,
Who does the mischief that is done
In everybody's house!
There's no one ever sees his face,
And yet we all agree
That every plate we break was cracked
By Mr. Nobody.'
Tis he who always tears out books,
Who leaves the door ajar,
He pulls the buttons from our shirts,
And scatters pins afar;
That squeaking door will always squeak,
For prithee, don't you see,
We leave the oiling to be done
By Mr. Nobody.
He puts damp wood upon the fire
That kettles cannot boil;
His are the feet that bring in mud,
And all the carpets soil.
The papers always are mislaid;
Who had them last, but he?
There's no one tosses them about
But Mr. Nobody.
The finger marks upon the door
By none of us are made;
We never leave the blinds unclosed,
To let the curtains fade.
The ink we never spill; the boots
That lying round you see
Are not our boots, — they all belong
To Mr. Nobody.

1. Which animal is Mr. Nobody compared to?
   (a) mouse   (b) cat
   (c) dog   (d) pig
2. What does Mr Nobody do to the books?
   (a) leaves them open
   (b) leaves them on the floor
   (c) tears them
   (d) hides them
3. What is the meaning of the word "prithee"?
   (a) pity
   (b) ancient way of saying please
   (c) pretty
   (d) someone's name
4. How does Mr. Nobody soil the carpets?
   (a) by spilling ink
   (b) by dropping food
   (c) by spilling paint
   (d) by his muddy feet
5. Which of these mischiefs does Mr. Nobody NOT do?
   (a) pulls buttons from shirts
   (b) soiling carpets
   (c) hitting birds with stones
   (d) spilling ink

XIII. Direction: This is the schedule for a five-day summer activity programme of Junior High School. Read the time table carefully and answer the questions that follow.

	DAY 1	DAY 2	DAY 3	DAY 4	DAY 5
Lesson 1 09.00-10.30	Introduction	Language and skills	Language and skills	Language and skills	Pronunciation Review
10.30-11.00	BREAK				
Lesson 2 11.00-12.00	Induction lesson	Pre-excursion	Project work		Pre-excursion
		Project work			Project work
12.30-13.45	LUNCH				
Afternoon 13.45-15.30	Activities	Half-day excursion		Culture class	

1. What is the duration of each day's Lesson 2?
   (a) one and a half hour
   (b) one hour
   (c) two hours
   (d) half an hour
2. How many times do the students get to do project work in the whole plan?
   (a) three   (b) two
   (c) one   (d) five
3. When do the students learn pronunciation?
   (a) Day 2   (b) Day 3
   (c) Day 5   (d) Day 4
4. When do the students do for an excursion?
   (a) Day 1   (b) Day 3
   (c) Day 4   (d) Day 2
5. How long are the students out for excursion?
   (a) one hour
   (b) one hour and 45 minutes
   (c) two hours
   (d) 45 minutes
6. What do the students do between 11.00 and 12.00 on Day 4?
   (a) project work   (b) activities
   (c) excursion   (d) review
7. What do the students do between 10.30 and 11.00 on Day 1?
   (a) activities
   (b) language and skills
   (c) lunch
   (d) break

Reading Comprehension

XIV. Read the news article and answer the questions that follow.

Child walks into borewell in Tamil Nadu

VELLORE, 29 Sept, 2013: A two-and-half-year boy accidentally fell into a 300-foot open borewell in a village in the Vellore district of Tamil Nadu on Sunday. Fire and rescue services personnel and police have launched rescue operations.

Police said Kutti, a farmer, his wife K Geetha and his two-and-half-year-old son K Rasan from Sivapuram visited his in-law's house at Koorampadi, near Arcot town.

The boy was playing in a farm belonging to one of his relatives, when he accidentally fell into a borewell at around 8 am on Sunday. His parents started to search for him when they found him missing. Later, they heard his screams from the borewell.

They sought the help of the villagers, who in turn alerted district officials and fire and rescue services personnel. A team reached the village with four excavators and began rescue operations. The child was trapped at around 30 feet in the 300-foot borewell which is six-and-half inch in diameter.

The rescue team proposes to seek the assistance of experts from Madurai and Coimbatore. District collector R Nanthagopal and superintendent of police P K Senthil Kumari were overseeing the rescue operations.

The borewell, which was dug a few days ago, was left open. The borewell diggers did not take any safety precautions.

1. What is the name of the boy who fell into the borewell?
   (a) Rasan
   (b) Kutti
   (c) Geetha
   (d) Rasam

2. How did the boy fall into the borewell?
   (a) Someone pushed him into it
   (b) He fell while playing
   (c) He decided to go down and explore
   (d) He was trying to rescue someone

3. When did the incident take place?
   (a) 8 am on Saturday
   (b) 9 am on Saturday
   (c) 8 am on Sunday
   (d) 9 am on Sunday

4. At what height was the child trapped?
   (a) 300 feet (b) 3,000 feet
   (c) 30 feet   (d) 3 feet

5. What is the name of the superintendent of police?
   (a) R Nanthagopal
   (b) K Geetha
   (c) Kutti
   (d) P K Senthil Kumari

6. The borewell was left open. This shows that the diggers were
   (a) careful
   (b) negligent
   (c) hard-working
   (d) inefficient

XV. Read the news article and answer the questions that follow.

NEW DELHI, 13 Aug, 2015: A mute stray dog called Pingu, usually seen as a nuisance, has become the unlikely hero of a locality in Delhi after he prevented a burglary and risked his life in the process.

Poornima Misra, the secretary of the Ashok Vihar colony's RWA and one of the few in the locality who didn't loathe the dog, has been feeding Pingu milk and biscuits for several years and said Pingu was a loyal dog that "does guard duty for free".

Things suddenly changed in the early hours of August 12. At about 1.30 am, recalled Misra, Pingu spotted a stranger climbing the stairs of a flat. Pingu must have attacked the burglar on a gut instinct — "he's generally a peaceful dog," according to Misra — and ripped a piece of cloth off his person.

To free himself, the thief may have pulled out a knife and slashed the dog's hind legs and escaped. Even though he was severely injured, Pingu managed to reach the guardhouse, approximately 200 metres from the area, leaving trails of blood everywhere.

"The guards were confused at first, and Pingu couldn't convey what had happened, as he is a mute dog — he doesn't bark," said Misra. His duty done, the dog collapsed due to the loss of blood and pain from the deep gashes. He was later given medical aid and is still recovering from his injuries.

Since the incident, the general attitude of the colony residents has changed towards Pingu, who garlanded him with a gold medallion. According to Misra, the residents have also become more amenable to stray dogs in general.

1. What is the physical disability that Pingu has?
    (a) He is blind   (b) He is mute
    (c) He is deaf   (d) He limps
2. What is the name of the colony where Pingu lives?
    (a) Vasant Kunj   (b) Ashok Nagar
    (c) Ashok Vihar   (d) Vasant Vihar
3. Which day did the incident take place?
    (a) 12 August   (b) 13 August
    (c) 14 August   (d) 15 August
4. How did the burglar injure Pingu?
    (a) Slashed his hind legs with a knife
    (b) Slashed his throat with a knife
    (c) Slashed his foreleg with a knife
    (d) Slashed his ear with a knife
5. How did the residents reward Pingu?
    (a) They gave him a gold medallion
    (b) They gave him a packet of biscuits
    (c) One of the residents took him home
    (d) They played with him

XVI. Read the news article and answer the questions that follow.

THANE, 3rd Sept, 2012: The sighting of an adult leopard led to panic in Ramnagar and Lokmanya Nagar settlements at the Yeoor hills here on Wednesday.

After residents reported the straying of the leopard into the locality from the woods, officials from the Sanjay Gandhi National Park arrived at the spot and searched the area for pugmarks. The search operation continued till late on Wednesday, but the leopard was not sighted.

Though the area is a protected forest, slums have encroached on forest property and have been provided with facilities like public transport, roads, water supply and electricity connection.

"We have been conducting awareness camps in these pockets and had asked locals to report any leopard spotting," Sandeep Yalgar, a forest official, said. "We received a call from the Ramnagar area and personnel from the BachaoKruti Dal rushed to the aid of the residents here."

Yalgar said the forest team would keep up the search for a couple of days.

The densely-populated slum settlements in Lokmanya Nagar locality of Wagle Estate often see leopards.

Recently, a cub had strayed from the forest and died after accidently falling into an abandoned well in the area.

Locals are extremely cautious about moving about in the area after dark.

Over the last decade, the Yeoor hills, the area along Ghodbunder Road and the forest area in Kolshet have seen encroachments by slums and multi-storey towers.

1. Where was the leopard sighted?
    (a) Yeshur Hills   (b) Yeoor Hills
    (c) Yashwant Hills   (d) Yeshu Hills
2. Who searched for pugmarks in the area?
    (a) Residents
    (b) Forest officials
    (c) Officials from Sanjay Gandhi National Park
    (d) Personnel from the BachaoKruti Dal
3. Recently which other animal had strayed into the locality?
    (a) A leopard cub
    (b) Adult leopard
    (c) A tiger
    (d) A hyena
4. Who rushed to help the residents as soon as the incident was reported?
    (a) Residents of neighbouring areas
    (b) Forest officials
    (c) Officials from Sanjay Gandhi National Park
    (d) Personnel from the BachaoKruti Dal

5. How long would the forest team keep up the search?
   (a) Two days
   (b) Two weeks
   (c) Two months
   (d) It was called off that day itself

XVII. Read the diary entry and answer the questions that follow.

Dear Diary,

Today is an exciting day. My younger sister Damini, my elder sister Janashree, my Dad, brother-in-law Deepak, my niece Diya and I are in Manali. This is our summer vacation for the week as a family. I really enjoy family vacations. This one is really nice because we didn't have to stay at a hotel, we are staying at the house of some relatives that Deepak has. We ate so much pizza because our relatives in here own a pizza store. We went walking down the mall road. The mall is actually a good place to get some shopping done. Damini got a nice dress that fit her just right. Her best friend's wedding is coming up so she bought the dress to wear it on that day. It was pink with a lot of glitter. I bought some shirts to wear at home. Janashree bought clothes for Diya. Deepak didn't buy anything because like any other guy, he does not have patience to go shopping. My Dad just walked around with us and did not buy anything at all. We also went to a party which was really fun. In the party Damini said she was tired and she did not dance. I was all over the dance floor. I really enjoy dancing. Janashree, Deepak and Dad were dancing as well. Damini was just sitting there. I think she was getting mad because she wanted to leave but Dad said she had to wait. We left really late and it was such a fun party. We recently got home and are ready to go to sleep after such a long day. In here, the night is actually beautiful because you can actually see the stars and everything is so calming. I think Manali is a really good place to relax and rest.

Good Night Diary

Pooja

1. How many took the trip to Manali?
   (a) Six   (b) Five
   (c) Four   (d) Seven

2. Whose relatives stay in Manali?
   (a) Damini   (b) Pooja
   (c) Pooja's Dad   (d) Deepak

3. Which of these describes the dress Damini bought?
   (a) Red with flowers
   (b) Pink with flowers
   (c) Pink with glitters
   (d) Red with glitters

4. Who did not buy anything from the mall?
   (a) Pooja and Janashree
   (b) Dad and Deepak
   (c) Deepak and Janashree
   (d) Deepak and Diya

5. Who did not dance at the party?
   (a) Damini   (b) Diya
   (c) Deepak   (d) Dad

6. What was going to be the duration of the trip?
   (a) 10 days   (b) 5 days
   (c) 7 days   (d) 15 days

HOTS

Read the passage carefully and answer the questions that follow.

Earth's Temperature

The world is now warmer than at almost any time since the end of the last ice age and, on present trends, will continue to reach a record high for the entire period since the dawn of civilisation, a study has found.

The study published in the journal Science, aims to give a global overview of Earth's temperatures over the past 11,300 years - a relatively balmy period known as the Holocene that began after the last major ice age ended and encompasses all of recorded human civilization.

Their data (compiled by studying such things as ice cores, fossils and ocean sentiment) looked back over a much longer era than previous research, which went back 1,500 years.

Scientists say it is further evidence that modern-day global warming isn't natural, but the result of rising carbon dioxide emissions that have rapidly grown since the Industrial Revolution began roughly 250 years ago. Scientists say that if natural factors were still governing the climate, the Northern Hemisphere would probably be destined to freeze over again in several thousand years. Instead, scientists believe the enormous increase in greenhouse gases caused by industrialization will almost certainly prevent that.

Shaun Marcott, a geologist at Oregon State University, says, "global temperatures are warmer than about 75 percent of anything we've seen over the last 11,000 years or so." The other way to look at that is, 25 percent of the time since the last ice age, it's been warmer than now.

It's taken just 100 years for the average temperature to rise by 1.3 degrees, when it took 5,000 years to do that before. By the end of the century, climate warming models predict an additional increase of 2 to 11.5 degrees, due largely to carbon emissions, the study noted.

1. 'Dawn' in this text means:
   (a) Heat   (b) Earth
   (c) Beginning   (d) Sunrise
2. 'Balmy' means:
   (a) Warm   (b) Cool
   (c) Cold   (d) Hot
3. The Earth's temperature has increased quickly since:
   (a) The Holocene
   (b) 1,500 years ago
   (c) The Northern Hemisphere
   (d) The Industrial Revolution
4. 'Prevent' means:
   (a) Complete   (b) Stop
   (c) Slow   (d) Encourage
5. This article could be described as a ___ look at the future.
   (a) Pessimistic   (b) Optimistic
   (c) Egoist   (d) Racist

SECTION 3
SPOKEN AND WRITTEN EXPRESSIONS

Agreement and Disagreement, Requests and Refusals

There are various ways in which people agree or disagree with each other while having an argument or discussion. A request has to be made politely, and a refusal or reservation against something can be expressed courteously as well.

Here are some ways to express these four sentiments, which help us in our daily English speech.

Agreement

When we agree with someone or something they say, these are a few ways in which we can express ourselves. There is no doubt about it.

Examples:

I completely/absolutely agree with you.
I agree with you entirely.
I totally agree with you.
I simply must agree with that.
I am of the same opinion.
That's exactly what I think.

Disagreement

Expressing disagreement is tougher than agreeing to something. Although honest, we must make sure that the expression is courteous and not offensive.

Examples:

I don't agree with you.
I'm sorry, but I disagree.
I'm afraid, I can't agree with you.
The problem is that I don't agree.
I doubt whether this is going to work.
With all due respect,
I am of a different opinion.
I don't share this / that / the view.
I have different thoughts about that.

Request

It is important to be polite when we request for something. Here are some ways of doing it.

Examples:

Can you show me your photo album, please?
Will you lend me your book, please?
Could you possibly show me the way to the post office, please?
Would you help me with this exercise, please?
Would you mind lending me your pen, please?
Remember, 'could' is more polite than saying 'can'.

Refusals

Sometimes people ask us to do things which we don't like or don't want to do. It is important to speak your mind and say "No". Here are some ways.

Strong Refusals
- No way
- Absolutely not
- No chance

Almost Certain Refusals
- Not likely
- I don't want to

Polite Refusals
- I'd rather not
- No, but thanks for asking

PRACTICE EXERCISE

I. Choose the correct option according to the task in the brackets.

1. I think *Shawshank Redemption* is one of the best movies ever made. (Agree)
   (a) I am of a different opinion.
   (b) No way!
   (c) Not likely.
   (d) There is no doubt about that.

2. I can't find Simba. You haven't seen her, have you? (Disagree)
   (a) No, I haven't.   (b) No, I didn't.
   (c) Yes, I have.   (d) Yes, I did.

3. _____ I speak to the principal, please? (Request)
   (a) Would   (b) Can
   (c) Won't   (d) Couldn't

4. Roller-coasters are fun. Do you want to ride with me? (Refuse strongly)
   (a) I don't think so.
   (b) Sure.
   (c) No way!
   (d) Let me think about it.

5. Look at the sky, I think it is going to rain. (Agree)
   (a) I'm sorry, but I disagree.
   (b) I think so too.
   (c) Absolutely not!
   (d) Not likely.

6. Summer is the best time to go for a picnic. (Disagree)
   (a) I'm sorry, but I disagree.
   (b) I doubt whether this is going to work.
   (c) I am of the same opinion.
   (d) That's exactly what I think.

7. _____ you like some more pie? (Request)
   (a) Can   (b) Could
   (c) Would   (d) Will

8. Would you like to go to see a movie tonight? (Refuse politely)
   (a) Okay. Sounds good.
   (b) Absolutely not!
   (c) Yeah. Good idea.
   (d) No, but thanks for inviting me.

9. Travelling around has become quite expensive. (Agree)
   (a) I don't think so.
   (b) I completely agree with you.
   (c) Really?
   (d) You must be mistaken.

10. Mrs Johnson is the best maths teacher in the school. (Disagree)
    (a) With all due respect, that's not what I think.
    (b) That's exactly what I think.
    (c) No
    (d) I am of the same opinion.

11. _____ buying some vegetables on your way home? (Request)
    (a) Could you
    (b) Will you
    (c) Would you
    (d) Would you mind

12. How about going skiing this weekend? (Refuse politely)
    (a) Great. What time?
    (b) Sorry. I'm busy this weekend.
    (c) Sounds like fun.
    (d) All right. When and where?

13. Could you lend me some money? (Refuse strongly)
    (a) No chance!
    (b) I'd rather not.
    (c) I disagree.
    (d) There is no doubt about it.

14. Betty, _____ help me with this grammar exercise, please? (Request)
    (a) can you
    (b) can't you
    (c) won't you
    (d) do you mind

15. The river is very dirty. People shouldn't have thrown household rubbish into the river. (Agree)
    (a) I am of a different opinion.
    (b) That's exactly what I think.
    (c) I have different thoughts about that.
    (d) I don't share this view.

II. Complete the following dialogues.

(i) Salil: Happy Birthday Meera! How old do you turn today?
Meera: Thanks a lot Salil. I turn 29 today.
Salil: Unbelievable. What is your beauty secret?
Meera: Nothing much. But I do believe that beauty is not just skin deep.
Salil: (1) _____ (Agree). I think we need to have a good personality more than good looks.
Meera: (2) _____ (Agree). That's why I keep an open mind.
Salil: (3) _____ (Agree).

(ii) Ria: Have you heard the latest album by the Boyband? I think the songs are really cool.
Ravish: (1) _____ (Disagree) I don't like the lyrcis at all.
Ria: You must listen to it once more, then you will like it.
Ravish: (2) _____ (Disagree) I don't think they are worth listening to twice.

(iii) Ashish: I think it's time we became business partners and opened a tuition centre together.
Anaya: (1) _____ (Agree) Many students and parents in and around our locality have been looking for a good tuition centre.
Ashish: Good. I was thinking of focusing exclusively on English.
Anaya : (2) _____ (Disagree) Most students opt for tuition centres that teach all subjects so that they don't have to move around a lot.

(iv) Boss: We really need to finish all the work related to this project as soon as possible. I know it's on a really short notice but (1)_____ (Request) work this weekend?
Employee: (2) _____ (Refuse politely). I have to attend my sister's wedding on Saturday.

(v) Stan: I have to meet a friend today at lunch. (1) _____(Request) covering for me till I return, in case the boss comes looking?
Betty: (2) _____ (Refuse strongly) I'm just going to say I don't know where you are.

Agreement and Disagreement, Requests and Refusals

HOTS

Choose the most appropriate option to agree or disagree, accept or reject the following expressions.

1. Someone says that your home football team will win their next match. You don't really agree and say:
   (a) I'm not quite sure. (b) I'm not real sure.
   (c) I'm not so sure. (d) None of these

2. Someone says something you disagree with. You say:
   (a) I don't agree. (b) I'm not agree.
   (c) I not agree. (d) None of these

3. Would you like another piece of chocolate cake – (Accept.)
   (a) No, thank you.
   (b) I'm afraid I'm on a diet.
   (c) Thank you, but I really can't eat any more.
   (d) Yes, please. It's delicious!

4. Please have some more fried chicken. (Refuse.)
   (a) I wouldn't say no.
   (b) Thank you, but I've had enough.
   (c) Thank you, you are very kind.
   (d) Yes, please. I'd love some.

5. We're having a party on Saturday. Would you like to come? (Accept.)
   (a) I'd love to!
   (b) I wish I could, but I really can't.
   (c) Sorry, I'll be busy on Saturday.
   (d) Thank you for the invitation, but I can't.

SECTION 4
ACHIEVERS' SECTION

Some Thoughtful Questions

1. Use the clues given below to complete this crossword puzzle.

Across
1. very tired
2. had an angry look on the face
3. short trousers
4. a fault in a machine that prevents it from working properly
5. a small and naughty boy-fairy

Down
6. work that must be done everyday, often boring
7. a basket with a lid
8. gave a short, high-pitched cry

Answer:

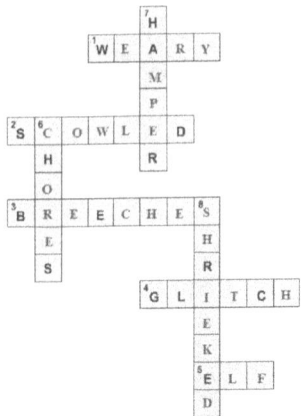

2. Look at this cartoon by R.K.Laxman. Read the sentence given below the cartoon and answer:
   - What is it about?
   - Do you find it funny? If so, why?
   - Do you think a cartoon is a serious drawing? Why or why not?

Get on with your homework — the sums, the composition, history, geography, chemistry, physics — and stop reading *The Laws Against Child Labour*!

Answer:
1. It depicts a father's concern for the betterment and improvement of his son.
2. Yes, the cartoon exhibits a funny tone. The father orders his son to finish his homework. But he stops the boy from reading the laws against child labour.
3. A cartoon mostly depicts the day-to-day activities of life with funny images. Although the above cartoon is a serious drawing, it draws our attention to a common problem that affects one and all.

3. **A summary of the story is given below. Fill in the blanks to complete it taking appropriate phrases from the box.**

   a dog, stronger than anyone else, the strongest of all, a wolf, the bear, afraid of man, his own master, a lion

This is the story of _____, who used to be _____. He decided to find a master _____. First he found _____, but the wolf was afraid of _____. The dog thought that the bear was _____. After some time the dog met _____, who seemed the strongest.

He stayed with the lion for a long time. One day he realized that the lion was _____. To this day, the dog remains man's best friend.

Answer:

This is the story of **a dog**, who used to be **his own master**. He decided to find a master **stronger than anyone else**. First he found **a wolf**, but the wolf was afraid of **the bear**. The dog thought that the bear was the **strongest of all**. After some time the dog met **a lion**, who seemed the strongest.

He stayed with the lion for a long time. One day he realized that the lion was **afraid of man**. To this day, the dog remains man's best friend.

4. **Word search**
   - There are twelve words hidden in this table.
   - Six can be found horizontally and the remaining six vertically.
   - All of them are describing words like 'good', 'happy', etc.
   - The first letters of the words are given below:

   Horizontal: H R F F S G
   Vertical: A W S F L Q

A	H	A	S	T	Y	D	U	L	M	N	P
N	F	L	U	V	Q	T	B	O	A	L	Z
G	Z	M	R	X	R	V	D	Y	F	Q	O
R	X	O	P	W	S	F	O	A	B	U	C
Y	C	P	R	E	A	D	Y	L	D	I	F
D	G	Q	I	Y	F	I	E	R	C	E	D
A	H	R	S	T	R	O	N	G	H	T	J
X	W	S	E	Z	E	A	B	H	K	S	K
G	O	O	D	A	E	C	A	I	J	T	L
F	R	I	G	H	T	E	N	E	D	W	M
B	S	J	C	B	L	D	F	J	K	X	V
E	E	K	D	E	M	B	E	L	M	U	Y

Answer:

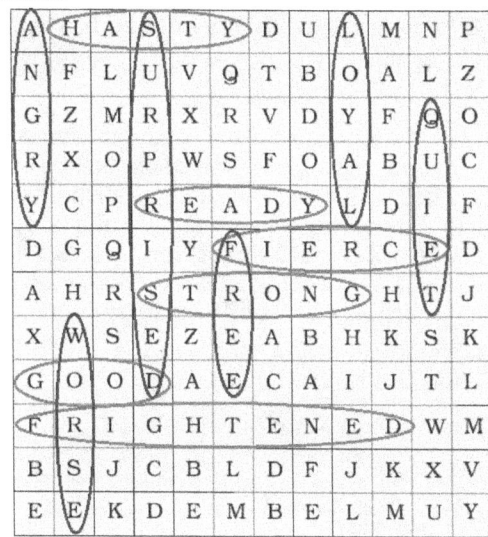

5. **Listen to these children. What are they talking about?**

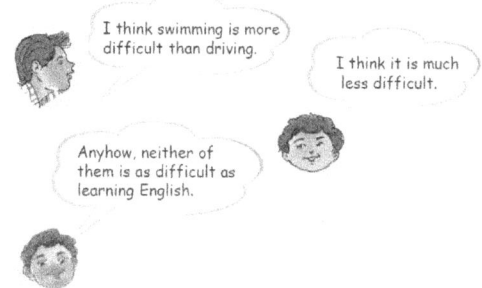

Answer:

The three boys are discussing their problems. The first boy considers swimming to be more difficult than driving. The second boy disagrees with it. He thinks that swimming is much less difficult than driving. However, the third boy thinks that learning English is the most difficult task in comparison to swimming and driving.

6. **Put these sentences from the story in the right order and write them out in a paragraph.**
   - I shall be so glad when today is over.
   - Having a leg tied up and hopping about on a crutch is almost fun, I guess.
   - I don't think I'll mind being deaf for a day — at least not much.
   - But being blind is so frightening.
   - Only you must tell me about things.

Some Thoughtful Questions

- Let's go for a little walk.
- The other bad days can't be half as bad as this.

Answer:

Let's go for a little walk. Only you must tell me about things. I shall be so glad when today is over. The other bad days can't be half as bad as this. Having a leg tied up and hopping about on a crutch is almost fun, I guess. I don't think I'll mind being deaf for a day — at least not much. But being blind is so frightening.

7. Given below is a page from a dictionary. Look at it carefully and

term noun
1 a fixed length of time. He was made captain of the football team for a **term** of one year.
2 a part of the school year. There are three **terms** in a school year.
terms plural noun the things you are asking for: If you agree to my **terms**—free meals and good wages—I will work for you.
terrace noun
1 a level area cut out from the side of a hill
2 a flat area outside a house. We sat on the **terrace** in the evening.
3 a row of houses joined together
terraced adjective. a **terraced** house
terrible adjective
1 causing fear. We saw a **terrible** storm.
2 very bad: Your writing is **terrible**.
terribly adverb It is **terribly** (= very) hot.
terrify verb
(present participle **terrifying**, past **terrified**) to fill with fear: The animals were **terrified** by the storm.
terror noun (no plural)
great fear: a feeling of **terror**
territory noun
(plural **territories**)
1 land ruled by one government: This island is British **territory**.
2 an area belonging to one person or animal. Wild animals will not allow other animals to enter their **territory**.
test¹ verb
1 to look at something to see if it is correct or will work properly: Before he bought the car, he drove it to **test** it.
2 to ask someone questions: The teacher **tested** the children on their homework.

test² noun
an examination: I passed my driving **test** today.
test tube noun small thin glass tube: We put chemicals in **test tubes** in our chemistry class.
text noun
1 the words used in a book
2 a few words from a book
textbook noun: A **textbook** is a book we use to learn about something.
than
(used when we compare things, in sentences like these): My brother is older **than** me. Mary sings better **than** anyone else in the class.
thank verb
to say we are grateful to someone: I **thanked** her for the present she sent me. **Thank you** for the present you sent me. No, **thank you**, I don't want any more tea.
thankful adjective very glad; grateful
thanks plural noun word to show that we are grateful: **Thanks** for helping me. It was **thanks** to John (= because of him) that we won the game.
that
1 (plural **those**) the one over there; the one further away from this one. This is my bowl. **that** bowl is yours.
2 (plural **those**) (used to point out someone or something used to mean the one known or mentioned already): Did you bring that photograph? We played football and **after that** (= next) we went home.
3 (used instead of **who, whom**)

(i) find a word which means the same as ghastly. Write down the word and its two meanings.
(ii) find a word meaning a part of the school year.
(iii) find a word that means examination.

Answer:

(i) **Ghastly:** terrible – causing fear, very bad
(ii) **Term:** a fixed length of time, a part of the school year
(iii) **Test:** to look at something to see if it is correct or will work properly, to ask someone questions

8. Replace the italicized portion of each sentence below with a suitable phrase from the box. Make necessary changes, wherever required.

look after, swallow, make it up, keep mum, go into, ease one's conscience, as ill luck would have it, a tight spot, take chances, my heart sank

1. The best way to avoid an unnecessary argument is to *remain silent*.
2. *Unfortunately*, the train I was trying to catch was cancelled.
3. He has been told not to take *risks* while driving a car through a crowded street.
4. He has been told not to *take risks* while driving a car through a crowded street.
5. The patient needs to be properly *taken care of*.
6. Why don't the two of you *end your quarrel* by shaking hands?
7. I was in a *difficult situation* till my friends came to my rescue.
8. When I saw a pile of dirty dishes, I *felt very disappointed*.
9. I will *examine* the matter carefully before commenting on it.
10. They criticized him in the meeting but he *accepted without protest* all the criticism.
11. It will *free me from worry* to know that I had done nothing wrong.

Answer:

1. The best way to avoid an unnecessary argument is to **keep mum**.
2. **As ill luck would have it**, the train I was trying to catch was cancelled.
3. He has been told not to take **chances** while driving a car through a crowded street.
4. He has been told not to **take chances** while driving a car through a crowded street.
5. The patient needs to be properly **looked after**.
6. Why don't the two of you **make it up** by shaking hands?
7. I was in **a tight spot** till my friends came to my rescue.
8. When I saw a pile of dirty dishes, **my heart sank.**
9. I will **go into** the matter carefully before commenting on it.
10. They criticized him in the meeting but he **swallowed** all the criticism.
11. It will **ease my conscience** to know that I had done nothing wrong.

9. **Match the following:**

Navigator	(a) Advises people what to do about jobs, personal problems, etc.
Architect	(b) Works in politics, usually by standing for election.
Politician	(c) Finds and monitors the route to get to a place, or the direction of travel.
Engineer	(d) Reports on recent news for newspaper, radio, or TV.
Computer Programmer	(e) Plans the design of a building, town or city.
Athlete	(f) Controls and puts together a programme of music.
Disk Jockey	(g) Works in sports or activities such as running, jumping, etc.
Composer	(h) Designs and builds things like roads, bridges or engines.
Counsellor	(i) Makes up notes to create music.
Journalist	(j) Designs the system by which a computer runs or gives information.

Answer:

Navigator	(c) Finds and monitors the route to get to a place, or the direction of travel.
Architect	(e) Plans the design of a building, town or city.
Politician	(b) Works in politics, usually by standing for election.
Engineer	(h) Designs and builds things like roads, bridges, or engines.
Computer Programmer	(j) Designs the system by which a computer runs or gives information.
Athlete	(g) Works in sports or activities such as running, jumping, etc.
Disk Jockey	(f) Controls and puts together a programme of music.
Composer	(i) Makes up notes to create music.
Counsellor	(a) Advises people what to do about jobs, personal problems, etc.
Journalist	(d) Reports on recent news for newspaper, radio or TV.

10. Look at your hands carefully. Now, write down for each finger one action for which that finger is particularly important. For example, the second (or index) finger helps to hold the knife down firmly when cutting.

    Answer:

    Thumb: It helps in holding a pen or pencil while writing.

    Second finger (Index finger): It helps in holding a knife while cutting vegetables or fruits.

    Third finger (Middle finger): It helps in sketching or holding a paintbrush while painting.

    Fourth finger (Ring finger): It is used for putting a ring on the finger and supports other fingers too.

    Fifth finger (Little finger/Pinky finger): It helps in supporting other fingers and making a fist.

Subjective Section

1. **Separate the Subject and the Predicate in the following sentences:**
   (a) The boy stood on the last bench.
   (b) The singing of the birds makes me happy.
   (c) A good boy passed the examination.
   (d) It is very hot.
   (e) The cow gives us milk.
   (f) The earth revolves round the sun.
   (g) Edison invented the phonograph.
   (h) Delhi is the capital of India.
   (i) We cannot make the ocean dry.
   (j) No man can serve two masters.

   Answer:

Subject	Predicate
The boy	stood on the last bench
The singing of the birds	makes me happy
A good boy	passed the examination
It	is very hot
The cow	gives us milk
The earth	revolves round the sun
Edison	invented the phonograph
Delhi	is the capital of India
We	cannot make the ocean dry
No man	can serve two masters

2. **Name the Part of Speech of each italicised word in the following sentences, giving in each case your reason for the classification:**
   (a) He *still* lives in that house.
   (b) The after effects of the drug are bad.
   (c) He told us all *about* the battle.
   (d) Suddenly one of the wheels came *off*.
   (e) Mohammedans *fast* in the month of Ramzan.
   (f) He kept the *fast* for a week.
   (g) He is *on* the committee.
   (h) Let us move *on*.
   (i) The *up* train is late.
   (j) I will watch *while* you sleep.

   Answer:
   (a) Adverb – adds something to the meaning of the verb 'lives'.
   (b) Adjective – adds something to the meaning of the noun 'effects'.
   (c) Preposition – shows the relation between 'all' and 'battle'.
   (d) Adverb – adds something to the meaning of the verb 'come'.
   (e) Verb – says something about 'Mohammedans'.
   (f) Noun – the name of something.
   (g) Preposition – shows the relation between 'he' and 'committee'.
   (h) Adverb – adds something to the meaning of the word 'move'.
   (i) Adjective – adds something to the meaning of the verb 'train'.
   (j) Conjunction – joins the two parts 'I will watch' and "you sleep'

3. **Pick out the Nouns in the following sentences and say whether they are Proper, Common, Material, Collective or Abstract.**
   (a) Raman is a good boy.
   (b) One should believe in truth.
   (c) A soldier is respected for his bravery.
   (d) Ornaments are made of gold and silver.
   (e) The case was decided by a bench of judges.
   (f) Mumbai is a big city.
   (g) The team won the match.
   (h) Blindness is the greatest curse.
   (i) Wisdom is better than strength.
   (j) This table is made of steel.

Answer:

Proper Nouns	Common Nouns	Material Nouns	Collective Nouns	Abstract Nouns
Raman, Mumbai	boy, one, soldier, ornaments, city, table	gold, silver, steel	bench, team	truth, bavery, blindness, wisdom, strength

4. **Change the following as directed :**
   (a) Birds fly in the sky. **(negative)**
   (b) Rohit loves his teacher. **(interrogative)**
   (c) Boys are doing their homework. **(negative)**
   (d) Yes, my friend speaks good English. **(interrogative)**
   (e) Dogs are barking. **(interrogative)**
   (f) He is learning music. **(negative)**
   (g) We are going to Kolkata soon. **(interrogative)**
   (h) Children play in the evening. **(negative)**
   (i) Ritu sings a song. **(negative)**
   (j) I am listening to western music. **(interrogative)**

   Answer:
   (a) Birds do not fly in the sky.
   (b) Does Rohit love his teacher?
   (c) Boys are not doing their homework.
   (d) Does your friend speak good English?
   (e) Are dogs barking?
   (f) He is not learning music.
   (g) Are we going to Kolkata soon?
   (h) Children do not play in the evening.
   (i) Ritu does not sing a song.
   (j) Am I listening to western music?

5. **Complete the sentences. Use one of these verbs:**

   build   cook   go   have   stand
   stay   swim   work   rain   watch

   (a) Please be quiet. I _____
   (b) Where is Umesh? He is in the kitchen. He _____
   (c) 'You _____ on my foot.'
   (d) Look! Somebody _____ in the river.
   (e) We're here on holiday. We _____ at the Royal Hotel.
   (f) Where's Renu? She _____ a shower.
   (g) They _____ a new theatre in the city centre at the moment.
   (h) I _____ now. Goodbye.
   (i) The weather is nice at the moment. It is not _____
   (j) You can turn off the television. I am not _____ it.

   Answer:
   (a) Please be quiet. I am *working*.
   (b) Where is Umesh? He is in the kitchen. He is *cooking*.
   (c) You are *standing* on my foot.
   (d) Look! Somebody is *swimming* in the river.
   (e) We're here on holiday. We are *staying* at the Royal Hotel.
   (f) Where's Renu? She is *having* a shower.
   (g) They are *building* a new theatre in the city centre at moment.
   (h) I am *going* now. Goodbye.
   (i) The' weather is nice at the moment. It is not *raining*.
   (j) You can turn off the television. I am not *watching* it.

6. **Fill in the blanks with the appropriate form (Present Continuous) of the verbs given in bracket.**
   (a) I am _____ the table **(turn)**.
   (b) Hari is _____ the juice **(suck)**.
   (c) Rani and Rajan _____ under the cot **(crawl)**.
   (d) The dog is _____ its tail **(wag)**.
   (e) You are _____ on your paper **(write)**.
   (f) She is _____ right hand **(wave)**.
   (g) He is _____ over the fence **(jump)**.
   (h) You are _____ your books **(take)**.
   (i) You are _____ the sweets in your mouth **(put)**.
   (j) Sita is _____ on her dress **(put)**.

   Answer:
   (a) I am *turning the table*.
   (b) Hari is *sucking* the juice.
   (c) Ravi and Rajan are *crawling* under the cot.
   (d) The dog is *wagging* its tail.
   (e) You are *writing* on your paper.

(f) She is *waving* her right hand.
(g) He is *jumping* over the fence.
(h) You are *taking* your books.
(i) You are *putting* the sweets in your mouth.
(j) Sita is *putting* on her dress.

7. **Fill in the blanks with the Present Perfect tense form of the verbs given in the brackets.**
   (a) The train _____ just now. **(arrive)**
   (b) I _____ not _____ the cinema all these years. **(visit)**
   (c) Someone _____ some crockery. **(break)**
   (d) I _____ never _____ the Taj **(see)**
   (e) I _____ not _____ him so far. **(meet)**
   (f) I _____ not _____ the work even now. **(finish)**
   (g) My friend _____ his purse, **(lose)**
   (h) They _____ my pen. **(take)**
   (i) Birds _____ from here, **(fly)**
   (j) Rachna _____ food, **(cook)**
   Answer:
   (a) The train *has arrived* just now.
   (b) I *have* not *visited* the cinema all these years.
   (c) Someone *has broken* some crockery.
   (d) I *have* never *seen* the Taj.
   (e) I *have* not *met* him so far.
   (f) I *have* not *finished* the work even now.
   (g) My friend *has lost* his purse.
   (h) They *have taken* my pen.
   (i) Birds *have flown* from here.
   (j) Rachna *has cooked* food.

8. **Fill in the blanks with the Present Perfect Continuous Tense of the verbs given in brackets.**
   (a) We _____ English for two years. (study)
   (b) He _____ in this school for several years. (teach)
   (c) I _____ in this flat since 2000. (live)
   (d) It _____ for three hours. (rain)
   (e) They _____ for seven hours. (work)
   Answer:
   (a) We have been studying English for two years.
   (b) He has been teaching in this school for several years.
   (c) I have been living in this flat since 2000.
   (d) It has been raining for three hours.
   (e) They have been working for seven hours.

9. **Put in a/an or the wherever necessary.**
   (a) Don't forget to turn off light when you go out.
   (b) Enjoy your holiday and don't forget to send me postcard.
   (c) What is name of this village?
   (d) Canada is very big country.
   (e) Which is largest city in Canada?
   (f) I like this room but I don't like colour of carpet.
   (g) Are you OK?' No, I have got headache'.
   (h) We live in old house near station.
   (i) What is name of director of film we saw last night?
   Answer:
   (a) Don't forget to turn off **the** light when you go out.
   (b) Enjoy your holiday and don't forget to send me **a** postcard.
   (c) What is **the** name of this village?
   (d) Canada is **a** very big country.
   (e) Which is **the** largest city in Canada?
   (f) I like this room but I don't like **the** colour of **the** carpet.
   (g) 'Are you OK? 'No, I have got **a** headache'.
   (h) We live in **an** old house near the station.
   (i) What is the name of **the** director of **the** film we saw last night?

10. **Change the following sentences from the active voice to the passive voice:**
    (a) The man cut down the tree.
    (b) Columbus discovered America.
    (c) His teacher praised him.
    (d) The boy teased the dog.
    (e) The police arrested him.
    (f) Rama was making a kite.
    (g) The boy caught the ball.
    (h) My father will write a letter.
    (i) I will defeat him.
    (j) He kept me waiting.
    (k) He scored twenty runs.
    (l) Manners reveal character.
    (m) Everyone loves him.
    (n) We expect good news.
    (o) I have sold my bicycle.
    (p) We must write to him.
    (q) They are doing the work.
    (r) The car hit the man.
    (s) Shyam eats an apple.

(t) I had posted the letter before I met him.
(u) How do they make coffee?
(v) Rachna had made tea.
(w) Abdul was watering the plants.
(x) Surabhi will write a letter.
(y) Mala has broken the window.

Answers:
(a) The tree was cut down by the man.
(b) America was discovered by Columbus.
(c) He was praised by his teacher.
(d) The dog was teased by the boy.
(e) He was arrested.
(f) A kite was being made by Rama.
(g) The ball was caught by the boy.
(h) A letter will be written by my father.
(i) He will be defeated by me.
(j) I was kept waiting.
(k) Twenty runs were scored by him.
(l) Character is revealed by manners.
(m) He is loved by everyone.
(n) Good news is expected.
(o) My bicycle has been sold.
(p) He must be written to by us.
(q) The work is being done by them.
(r) The man was hit by the car.
(s) An apple is eaten by Shyam.
(t) The letter had been posted (by me) before I met him.
(u) How is coffee made?
(v) Tea had been made by Rachna.
(w) Plants were being watered by Abdul.
(x) A letter will be written by Surabhi.
(y) The window has been broken by Mala.

11. **Re-arrange the following words/phrases to make meaningful sentences:**

I. (a) control/over/self-control is/exercised/self/one's
(b) power/it/having/emotions/one's/mind/and/control/under/is/the/of
(c) clears/it/strengthens/mind/the/and/will-power
(d) elevates/it/character/our
(e) gives/freedom/it/us/peace/joy/and/bliss

II. (a) bring/ festivals / life / colours / to / the / human / of/ a
(b) many/festivals/celebrated/in/types/India/of/are
(c) these/Holi/some/Diwali/of/are/Id/Christmas/and
(d) festival/Holi/the/colours/is/of
(e) celebrated/India/it/over/all/is

III. (a) peacock/a/beautiful/is/a/bird
(b) neck/feathers/covered/is/lovely/its/with
(c) green/blue/its/and/body/is
(d) glory/its/tail/long/is/its
(e) it/national/our/is/bird.

IV. (a) called/rose/the/queen/the/is/flowers/of
(b) widely/it/grown/is/the/all/world/over
(c) 500/there/about/are/species/roses/of
(d) the/rose/persian/best/is/the
(e) brought/from / there / was /it/ India/to

V. (a) person/a/healthy/exercise/makes
(b) important /in/ life / it/ one's /is
(c) exercises/physical/person/make/physically/a/fit
(d) mental/makes/fresh/the/exercise/mind
(e) mind/it/sharp/makes/the/too.

VI. (a) keep/yitamins/fit/body/our.
(b) appetite/they/and/improve/body's/increase/ability/fight/to/diseases
(c) help/minerals/growth/the/body/of/in/the
(d) vegetables/fresh fruits/sources/and/are/vitamins/of/minerals/and
(e) roughage/body/helps/undigested/get rid of/to/the/food

VII. (a) useful/camel/is/animal/desert/the/most/the/in/the
(b) heavy/it/ through/ carry/ can/loads/ sand /hot

(c) feet/adapted/walk/are/its/to/sand/on
(d) without/live/it/water/food/many days/can/an/for
(e) the ship of the desert/camel/called/is/the

VIII. (a) India's/kabaddi/one/is /games/indigenous/of
(b) popular/rural/it/in/is/areas
(c) does not/playground/this/require game/large/a
(d) is/it/game/cheap/very/a
(e) played/it/courtyard/can/in/be/even/the/of/house/a

IX. (a) nurse/symbol/is/a/of/humanity/service/a/and
(b) frequently / she / seen/hospitals /is / in
(c) attentive/she/her/very/remains/duties/to
(d) noble/she/patients/all/is/to
(e) she/popularly/is/as/known/sister

X. (a) Vindhya hills/located/in/Madhya Pradesh/the Bandhavgarh National Park/ the/is/of
(b) tigers / natural / it / home /is / for / a / protected
(c) also/other/found/animals/here/are
(d) rare birds/spotted/also/some/can/be
(e) great/wildlife lovers/place/is/for/it/a

Answers:
I. (a) Self-control is control exercised over one's self.
(b) It is the power of having one's emotions and mind under control.
(c) It clears mind and strengthens will power.
(d) It elevates our character.
(e) It gives us freedom, peace, bliss and joy.

II. (a) Festivals bring colours to the life of a human.
(b) In India many types of festivals are celebrated.
(c) Some of these are Holi, Diwali, Id and Christmas.
(d) Holi is the festival of colours.
(e) It is celebrated all over India.

III. (a) A peacock is a beautiful bird.
(b) Its neck is covered with lovely feathers.
(c) Its body is green and blue.
(d) Its glory is its tail.
(e) It is our national bird.

IV. (a) The rose is called the queen of flowers.
(b) It is widely grown all over the world.
(c) There are about 500 species of roses.
(d) The persian rose is the best.
(e) From there it was brought to India.

V. (a) Exercise makes a person healthy.
(b) It is important in one's life.
(c) Physical exercises make a person physically fit.
(d) Mental exercise makes the mind fresh.
(e) It makes the mind sharp too.

VI. (a) Vitamins keep our body fit.
(b) They improve appetite and increase body's ability to fight diseases.
(c) Minerals help in the growth of the body.
(d) Fresh fruits and vegetables are sources of vitamins and minerals.
(e) Roughage helps the body to get rid of undigested food.

VII. (a) The camel is the most useful animal in the desert.
(b) It can carry heavy loads through hot sand.
(c) Its feet are adapted to walk on sand.
(d) It can live without food and water for many days.
(e) The camel is called the ship of the desert.

VIII. (a) Kabaddi is one of India's indigenous games.
(b) It is popular in rural areas.
(c) This game does not require a large playground.
(d) It is a very cheap game.
(e) It can be played even in the courtyard of a house.

IX. (a) A nurse is a symbol of service and humanity.
(b) She is frequently seen in hospitals.
(c) She remains very attentive to her duties.
(d) She is noble to all patients.
(e) She is popularly known as sister.

X. (a) The Bandhavgarh National park is located in the Vindha hills of Madhya Pradesh.
(b) It is a natural protected home for tigers.
(c) Other animals are also found here.
(d) Some rare birds can also be spotted.
(e) It is a great place for wildlife lovers.

12. **Unseen passage. Read and answer the questions that follows:**

Sachin Tendulkar was born on 24 April 1973. He was one of the best batsmen and was also called the God of Cricket.

He was awarded, Bharat Ratna, India's highest civilian award in 2014. Moreover, he received many awards like Arjuna Award, Padma Shri Award, Padma Vibhushan Award, etc.

He scored more than 14,000 runs in his cricket career. Presently, he is associated with an organization named Apnalaya.

In this organization, he takes care of the upbringing of about 200 children. There is a film related to his life. The name of the film is Sachin: A Billion Dreams which was released in 2017.

The film was directed by James Erskine.

Questions:
(a) In which year was the film released?
(b) What is Apnalaya?
(c) How many runs did Sachin score in his cricket career?
(d) When was Sachin Tendulkar born?
(e) Write any two names of his awards.

Answers
(a) The film was released in 2017.
(b) Apnalaya is an organization that is taken care of by Sachin Tendulkar.
(c) Sachin Tendulkar scored more than 14,000 runs in his cricket career.
(d) Sachin Tendulkar was born on 24 April 1973.
(e) Bharat Ratna and Padma Shri Award.

13. **Arrange the jumbled words in the following questions punctuate them correctly, and write the complete sentence in the space given below.**
(a) These favorite my colours purple, turquoise, pink and yellow are.:
_____
(b) Speech your cheat notes; you won't need your memorize.
_____
(c) What doing ? are you teacher asked the. " "
_____
(d) How are morning! you good?
_____
(e) Fish pulled, the caught having out the of he it the net
_____

Answer:
(a) These are my favourite colorus: purple, turquoise, pink, and yellow.
(b) Memorize your speech; you won't need your cheat notes.
(c) "What are you doing?", asked the teacher.
(d) Good morning! How are you?
(e) Having caught the fish, he pulled it out of the net.

14. **Change the following sentences from direct to indirect speech and rewrite them in the given space.**
(a) "Do you want to know the secret?" he asked me.
_____
(b) "Hello! Can I come in?" He asked me.
_____
(c) The girl said, "It gives me great pleasure to be here this evening."
_____
(d) He said, "Let's wait for her return."
_____
(e) My father enquired, "Are you ready to go?"
_____

Subjective Section

Answer:
(a) He asked me whether I wanted to know the secret.
(b) He greeted me and asked if he could come in.
(c) The girl said that it gave her great pleasure to be there that evening.
(d) He urged us to wait for her return.
(e) My father asked if I was ready to go.

15. **Change the following sentences into direct speech and rewrite them in the space given below.**
    (a) He asked her what she wanted.
    _____
    (b) She said that Singapore was green and clean.
    _____
    (c) He asked if he could come in.
    _____
    (d) He said that I might need it.
    _____
    (e) John said that he supposed that he had lost his watch there.
    _____

Answer:
(a) "What do you want?" he said to her.
(b) She said, "Singapore is green and clean."
(c) "Can I come in?," he enquired.
(d) He said, "you might need it."
(e) John said, "I suppose I lost my watch here."

Model Test Paper 1

I. **Select the correct option that identifies the nouns in the following sentences.**

1. It will take all of your energy.
   (a) Take (b) All
   (c) Your (d) Energy
2. The works of many great poets have been placed on reserve.
   (a) Many (b) Great
   (c) Placed (d) Reserve
3. The Brooklyn Bridge was opened in 1883.
   (a) Bridge (b) Was
   (c) Opened (d) In
4. Sparta and Athens were enemies during the Peloponnesian War.
   (a) And (b) Were
   (c) During (d) War
5. The skeletons of these fish are made of cartilage rather than bone.
   (a) Made (b) Rather
   (c) Their (d) Bone

II. **Fill in the blanks with the correct form of verbs.**

1. The swimming pool _____ at 9 a.m. and _____ at 6.30 p.m. daily.
   (a) is opening / is closing
   (b) opens / closes
   (c) has opened / has closed
   (d) opened / closed
2. The Olympic Games _____ place every four years.
   (a) have taken (b) are taking
   (c) take (d) took
3. Look! That man _____ to open the door of your car.
   (a) tries (b) has been trying
   (c) tried (d) is trying
4. The river _____ much faster than usual.
   (a) flows (b) has been flowing
   (c) is flowing (d) flowed
5. We usually _____ vegetables in our garden but this year we _____ any.
   (a) are growing / don't grow
   (b) grew / haven't grown
   (c) grow / aren't growing
   (d) grow / don't grow

III. **Fill in the blanks with the correct phrasal verbs.**

1. There are 100 applicants for every vacancy; so it's not very easy to _____ them.
   (a) call (b) get
   (c) put (d) give
2. I don't think I'll get the job but I decided to _____ STET an application anyway.
   (a) set (b) put
   (c) come (d) call
3. Things were going very badly; so we decided to _____ an outside consultant.
   (a) give (b) take
   (c) come (d) call
4. The joint venture you are proposing is very interesting and we would really like to _____ on it.
   (a) set (b) come
   (c) put (d) give
5. I tried to resist his arguments but in the end I had to _____ in on that point.
   (a) give (b) take
   (c) be (d) get

IV. **Fill in the blanks with suitable adverbs.**

1. I found his house very _____.
   (a) easily (b) difficultly
   (c) frequently (d) none of these
2. Rohan behaves very _____ with his elders.
   (a) goodly (b) badly
   (c) easily (d) none of these
3. My father will be _____ of town this weekend.
   (a) inside (b) outside
   (c) out (d) none of these

4. Rohan plays football _____.
   (a) aggressively   (b) sympathetically
   (c) hardly   (d) none of these
5. He doesn't care for anything and _____ looks happy every time.
   (a) since   (b) ago
   (c) hence   (d) none of these

V. Fill in the blanks with suitable articles.
1. The only sport we enjoy is _____ hockey.
   (a) a   (b) an
   (c) the   (d) none of these
2. I left it at _____ office.
   (a) the   (b) an
   (c) a   (d) none of these
3. He is _____ doctor.
   (a) an   (b) a
   (c) the   (d) none of these
4. He drives at a speed of 90 miles _____ hour.
   (a) a   (b) an
   (c) the   (d) none of these
5. It's in _____ Arthur Road.
   (a) a   (b) an
   (c) the   (d) none of these

VI. Fill in the blanks with suitable prepositions.
1. There is no use _____ going there at this time.
   (a) at   (b) of
   (c) on   (d) off
2. He complains _____ headache.
   (a) of   (b) off
   (c) from   (d) about
3. They went to Agra _____ bus.
   (a) of   (b) in
   (c) by   (d) from
4. I am writing this essay _____ blue ink.
   (a) in   (b) with
   (c) from   (d) on
5. She has three children _____ her first husband.
   (a) of   (b) in
   (c) by   (d) from

VII. Choose the correct passive voice of the given sentences.
1. Anil Sharma makes tea.
   (a) Tea is made by Anil Sharma.
   (b) Tea is made by the Anil Sharma.
   (c) Tea was made by Anil Sharma.
   (d) Tea has made by Anil Sharma.
2. My father loves me.
   (a) I loved my father.
   (b) I was loved by my father.
   (c) I were loved by my father.
   (d) I am loved by my father.
3. We hate him.
   (a) He has hated by us.
   (b) He is hated by us.
   (c) He was hated by us.
   (d) He will hated by us.
4. Savita does not like me.
   (a) I am not like by Savita.
   (b) I am not liked by Savita.
   (c) I was not liked by Savita.
   (d) I were not liked by Savita.
5. He is making a film.
   (a) A film is made by him.
   (b) A film had being made by him.
   (c) A film is being made by him.
   (d) A film has being made by him.

VIII. Choose the correct narration of the following sentences.
1. He said to me, "I am ready".
   (a) He told to me that he is ready.
   (b) He told me that he was ready.
   (c) He told me that I am ready.
   (d) He told me that I will ready.
2. Sonia said, "You help my sister".
   (a) Sonia said that I helps her sister.
   (b) Sonia asked me to help her sister.
   (c) Sonia said that I helped her sister.
   (d) Sonia says that I helped her sister.
3. They said, "We cannot live without oxygen".
   (a) They said that we cannot live without oxygen.
   (b) They said that they cannot live without oxygen.
   (c) They said that they would not live without oxygen.
   (d) They says that they cannot live without oxygen.
4. Rahul said to me, "We are mortal".
   (a) Rahul said to me that we are mortal.
   (b) Rahul says to me that we are mortal.
   (c) Rahul said to me that we all are mortal.
   (d) Rahul said to me that he and I are mortal.

5. The Indian Express says, "We shall issue an astrology section in our Thursday's paper".
   (a) The Indian express says that it will issue a astrology section in their Thursday's paper.
   (b) The Indian express says that they will issue a astrology section in their Thursday's paper.
   (c) The Indian express said that it will issue a astrology section in its Thursday's paper.
   (d) The Indian express says that it will issue an astrology section in its Thursday's paper.

IX. **Read the passage carefully and answer the questions that follow.**

The horse is very useful animal. It is found in almost every country. It feeds on grass or gram. It is therefore, used for riding over long distances. It is used in the cities for carrying luggage by cart. An Arabian horse is world famous. It is used by the military to carry soldiers. It is also used in sports. Horse racing and polo are very popular sports in which horse plays a part.

1. What does the horse feed on?
   (a) Meal   (b) Grass
   (c) Pulse   (d) Grains
2. How is the horse used in cities?
   (a) Uploading luggage
   (b) Sending luggage
   (c) Carrying luggage
   (d) None of these
3. Which horse is used in military?
   (a) Indian   (b) Russian
   (c) Iranian   (d) Arabian
4. Write your own sentence with
   Popular: _____
5. Name two games where horses play a part.
   (a) _____
   (b) _____

X. **Choose the most appropriate options to agree or disagree, accept or reject the following expressions.**

1. Your friend says, "Let's go out tonight" and you think it's a good idea. You say:
   (a) I agree.   (b) I'm agree.
   (c) I'm agreeing.   (d) None of these
2. Your friend asks, "What about getting a pizza tonight" You think it's a good idea and say:
   (a) I agree to you.
   (b) I agree with you.
   (c) I'm not sure.
   (d) None of these
3. You and a friend want to buy a birthday present for another friend. You suggest buying tickets for a concert then ask your friend:
   (a) Are you agree?
   (b) Do you agree?
   (c) Do you think I'm right?
   (d) None of these
4. Someone says, "It's cold today" and you agree. You say:
   (a) You're right!
   (b) You've right!
   (c) You so right!
   (d) None of these
5. Your friend is talking about a film you both saw and says it was fantastic. You agree and say:
   (a) I absolute agree.
   (b) I completely agree.
   (c) I agree up for a point.
   (d) None of these

Model Test Paper 2

Choose the best word/phrase to complete each sentence.

1. The tiger _____ is decreasing rapidly.
   (a) calculation (b) circulation
   (c) population (d) education

2. Ram and Kumar have had a fight, they _____ spoken to each other for the last two weeks.
   (a) will be (b) can't
   (c) aren't (d) haven't

3. What's all that noise? What's _____?
   (a) occurring (b) happening
   (c) going (d) playing

4. What is a doctor's job?
   (a) He promises. (b) He insists.
   (c) He prescribes. (d) He proposes.

5. When Steven broke his car's windscreen while playing cricket, his father _____.
   (a) hit the roof (b) hit the ball
   (c) hit the road (d) hit the sack

6. Hockey players earn _____ money than cricket players.
   (a) fewer (b) less
   (c) little (d) few

7. I don't remember _____ before an exam. My mind goes blank.
   (a) everything (b) something
   (c) nothing (d) anything

8. We should drink _____ water during the summer.
   (a) full of (b) a lot of
   (c) too many (d) much

9. Sohail doesn't _____ along with his little sister. They are always arguing.
   (a) go (b) carry
   (c) get (d) keep

10. When the wildlife experts _____ that the tiger population was decreasing they started the 'save the tiger' campaign.
    (a) discovered (b) unwrapped
    (c) explored (d) diagnosed

How many words are wrongly spelt in the sentences below?

11. The nurcewraped a bandege round his head.
    (a) 1 (b) 2
    (c) 3 (d) None

12. He tried to brake the bad habit but unfortunately all his efforts have been in vein.
    (a) 3 (b) 2
    (c) 1 (d) None

13. One should never loose ones patience.
    (a) 1 (b) 2
    (c) 3 (d) None

Choose the best answer to complete each sentence from the options given.

14. _____ by bus is cheaper than by taxi in a city.
    (a) Driving (b) Riding
    (c) Tripping (d) Commuting

15. When the tiger roars in the jungle; all the elephants _____.
    (a) howl (b) growl
    (c) trumpet (d) scream

16. I'm on holiday, my daily schedule is quite _____ we can arrange to meet any time.
    (a) adjustable (b) flexible
    (c) elastic (d) stretchable

17. During the floods the military constructed a temporary floating _____ over the river.
    (a) pontoon bridge (b) flyover
    (c) bridge (d) draw bridge

18. His father works in a company which was the first to _____ Compact discs (CDs) in the 1970s.
    (a) construct   (b) fabricate
    (c) create   (d) invent
19. Let's have a Chinese _____ tonight – I'm not in the mood to cook.
    (a) take away
    (b) take in
20. His father used to work overtime to _____ money for his education.
    (a) gain   (b) win
    (c) raise   (d) achieve
21. In spite of telling him how to do it again and again he made _____ mistake.
    (a) many   (b) yet another
    (c) all   (d) little
22. I'm going to Singapore for _____ day or two.
    (a) some   (b) the
    (c) a   (d) none of these
23. It was raining and I was _____ late for school.
    (a) greatly   (b) by an hour
    (c) entirely   (d) almost
24. Her hair wasn't real. She was wearing a _____.
    (a) hair color   (b) wig
    (c) curls   (d) hair pin
25. What does 'it slipped my mind' mean?
    (a) Forgot to do something
    (b) Just remembered to do something
    (c) Something went passed my head
    (d) Cannot understand anything
26. Ali promised to give her a lift if it _____.
    (a) is rained   (b) will rain
    (c) rained   (d) rains
27. It was very hot. _____, I put on the air conditioner.
    (a) Even though   (b) But
    (c) Even   (d) Even so
28. I _____ you can write so neatly and I can't.
    (a) am hating   (b) hate
    (c) hate that   (d) hate it
29. I have a toy aeroplane _____ a remote control.
    (a) which with   (b) which has
    (c) has   (d) having
30. You should eat some breakfast before you _____ in the morning.
    (a) left   (b) will leave
    (c) had left   (d) leave
31. Wow! These apples are very tasty, and they were _____ ones I could find.
    (a) cheapest   (b) the cheapest
    (c) cheap   (d) the cheap
32. If I _____ press this round button, will it start playing the movie?
    (a) will   (b) —
    (c) could   (d) would

SECTION-II : READING

Read each passage and answer the questions that follow.

Every year large numbers of plastic bottles wash up on the beaches. However, this problem can be solved if the new plan is brought in, as suggested by the scientists. In the new scheme, fishermen will be encouraged to round up plastic bottles with their fishing nets. They can then sell these and cash in on the rising price of old plastic. The recycling centres can then turn toxic waste into packaging. Scientists believe, this scheme will compensate fishermen for the loss of income due to more and more people turning vegetarian. Scientists aim to bring in this scheme soon before the fishermen are forced to sell their boats.

33. What does, 'bottles wash up on the beach' mean?
    (a) Bottles are washed on the beach.
    (b) Bottles arrive on the shore, carried by the waves.
    (c) Beach is washed by the bottles.
    (d) Bottles are left behind by people visiting the beach.

Model Test Paper

34. Old plastic is made into useful things in a _____.
    (a) fishing net   (b) science lab
    (c) recycling centre   (d) beach
35. What is the new scheme?
    (a) Fishermen gather plastic bottles and sell them.
    (b) Fishermen encourage scientists to use fishing nets.
    (c) Fishermen are encouraged to make a circle with the nets.
    (d) Fishermen use fishing nets to make around bottle.
36. Which word in the second paragraph means 'changing habits'?
    (a) Compensate   (b) Forced
    (c) Turning   (d) Income

Sharks

There are many types of sharks found in the oceans around the world. Some of them are very big while others are quite small. You need to be scared of some while others are very calm like the Zebra shark. They are small, gentle shark that can be kept in an aquarium with other fish.

You may be surprised to learn that some of the largest species of sharks in the ocean are the nicest ones to encounter. There are 360 different species of sharks in the world. Some of the sharks we should be scared of are e.g. the Great White Sharks. They have attacked more people than any other shark. Their average length is about 12 feet and weighs about 3,000 pounds. Great white sharks are also different from others because they can lift their heads out of the water. Similar to them in length are the Blue sharks. Blue sharks are the fastest swimming sharks and can even leap out of the water and they can eat almost anything and have attacked people too. Tiger sharks too have attacked people but they come second to Great white shark in attacking people. A different type of shark which can swim in salt and fresh water is Bull shark. It comes after the Blue shark in order, for the number of attacks on people.

37. Which shark does not kill fish or people?
    (a) Blue shark   (b) Bull shark
    (c) Zebra shark   (d) Tiger shark
38. In attacking people which shark comes second of all?
    (a) Great white shark   (b) Blue shark
    (c) Bull shark   (d) Tiger shark
39. Which shark can jump out of the water?
    (a) Great white shark   (b) Blue shark
    (c) Bull shark   (d) Tiger shark
40. Which shark's average length is 12 feet?
    (a) Great white shark   (b) Bull shark
    (c) Zebra shark   (d) Tiger shark

SECTION-III :
Spoken and written expression

Choose the best response to complete each conversation.

41. Steve : I live in a big city.
    Jill : _____.
    (a) I live near the park.
    (b) So do I.
    (c) This place is crowded.
    (d) I also.
42. Robin : Have they got a house in the city too?
    Sam : _____
    (a) Yes, they have.
    (b) Yes, they do.
    (c) Yes, have got.
    (d) Yes, they do have.
43. Imran : Jay has already eaten two burgers, but he is still hungry.
    Sam : Ok, I will give him _____ burger.
    (a) some   (b) other
    (c) any   (d) another
44. Clair : We both did an equal amount of work, but he was paid more money than I was.
    Bob : _____.
    (a) That's average.
    (b) That's not enough.
    (c) That's funfair.
    (d) That's not fair.
45. 'My computer crashed and I lost all my photos.'
    (a) 'I don't think I can replace any photos.'
    (b) 'I don't think I can restore any photos.'
    (c) 'I don't think I can recover any photos.'
    (d) 'I don't think I can remake any photos.'

46. Ram : 'You are _____ hard today.'
    Kumar : 'Yes, I have an exam tomorrow.'
    (a) studying (b) staying
    (c) to sleep (d) sleeping

47. Sonia : 'I can't understand what you are saying.'
    (a) 'Could you speak slowlier please.'
    (b) 'Could you speak more slowly please.'
    (c) 'Could you speak down please.'
    (d) 'Could you speak low please.'

48. Vikram : 'I was waiting for your call all day yesterday.'
    Sonia : 'Sorry, I had a bit of a problem _____ through.'
    (a) phoning (b) passing
    (c) calling (d) getting

49. What is the indirect speech of the sentence.
    Ali said, 'I'm working on the science project'.
    (a) Ali said that he will be working on the science project.
    (b) Ali said that he is working on the science project.
    (c) Ali said that he was working on the science project.
    (d) Ali said that he had worked on the science project.

50. 'You are probably sleepy, because you _____.'
    (a) are yawning a lot.
    (b) went out for lunch.
    (c) ate too much chocolates.
    (d) watched a movie.

Model Test Paper

Answer Keys

Scan the QR Code to see the Hints and Solutions

Access Content Online on Dropbox: https://www.dropbox.com/scl/fi/x1il8nzpuzwm1qyz8yycu/NSO-01-Science-Olympiad-Hints-and-Solutions.pdf?rlkey=kzkx1753ie7dfs4rlkt3yo4pa&dl=0

SECTION 1: WORD AND STRUCTURE KNOWLEDGE

1. NOUN

Answer Key

I

1. (b)	2. (b)	3. (a)	4. (c)	5. (b)	6. (d)	7. (b)	8. (b)	9. (a)	10. (b)
11. (a)	12. (a)	13. (b)	14. (b)	15. (b)					

II

1. (b)	2. (a)	3. (a)	4. (d)	5. (c)	6. (b)	7. (c)	8. (d)	9. (a)	10. (d)
11. (b)	12. (a)	13. (b)	14. (d)	15. (b)					

III

1. (a)	2. (c)	3. (a)	4. (c)	5. (b)	6. (a)	7. (b)	8. (c)	9. (a)	10. (b)

HOTS

I

1. (d)	2. (a)	3. (d)	4. (d)	5. (d)

II

1. (c)	2. (d)	3. (a)	4. (a)	5. (d)

2. PRONOUN

Answer Key

I

1. (a)	2. (d)	3. (b)	4. (a)	5. (b)	6. (d)	7. (b)	8. (b)	9. (c)	10. (c)
11. (a)	12. (c)	13. (c)	14. (a)	15. (a)					

II

1. (a)	2. (b)	3. (d)	4. (a)	5. (d)	6. (b)	7. (a)	8. (d)	9. (c)	10. (a)

III

1. (a)	2. (b)	3. (c)	4. (a)	5. (b)	6. (c)	7. (a)	8. (b)	9. (a)	10. (c)
11. (d)	12. (a)	13. (b)	14. (b)	15. (c)					

HOTS

1. (d)	2. (b)	3. (a)	4 I. (b)	4 II. (c)
4 III. (c)	4 IV. (d)			

3. ADJECTIVES

Answer Key

I

1. (d)	2. (a)	3. (c)	4. (a)	5. (a)

II

1. (c)	2. (a)	3. (b)	4. (d)	5. (c)	6. (a)	7. (b)	8. (c)	9. (a)	10. (d)
11. (b)	12. (c)	13. (b)	14. (d)	15. (a)					

III

1. (b)	2. (a)	3. (c)	4. (d)	5. (d)	6. (c)	7. (b)	8. (a)	9. (b)	10. (a)

HOTS

1. (a)	2. (b)	3. (c)	4. (b)	5. (c)

4. ARTICLES

Answer Key

I

1. (a)	2. (c)	3. (c)	4. (b)	5. (d)	6. (c)	7. (a)	8. (a)	9. (d)	10. (a)
11. (a)	12. (b)	13. (b)	14. (a)	15. (b)	16. (a)	17. (d)	18. (b)	19. (d)	20. (a)

II

1. (a)	2. (c)	3. (b)	4. (a)	5. (c)	6. (c)	7. (d)	8. (a)	9. (a)	10. (b)

HOTS

1. (d)	2. (d)	3. (c)	4. (c)	5. (b)	6. (c)	7. (d)	8. (c)	9. (c)	10. (d)

5. VERB

Answer Key

I

1. (c)	2. (a)	3. (d)	4. (c)	5. (d)	6. (a)	7. (b)	8. (c)	9. (a)	10. (a)

II

1. (b)	2. (d)	3. (c)	4. (c)	5. (a)	6. (c)	7. (b)	8. (a)	9. (b)	10. (b)

III

1. (b)	2. (b)	3. (c)	4. (a)	5. (d)	6. (b)	7. (d)	8. (d)	9. (a)	10. (b)

IV

1. (a)	2. (b)	3. (d)	4. (a)	5. (b)	6. (a)	7. (c)	8. (b)	9. (a)	10. (b)

HOTS

I

| 1. (a) | 2. (b) | 3. (c) | 4. (d) | 5. (c) |

II

| 1. (d) | 2. (c) | 3. (a) | 4. (a) | 5. (a) |

6. ADVERB

Answer Key

I

| 1. (b) | 2. (b) | 3. (d) | 4. (c) | 5. (a) | 6. (c) | 7. (a) | 8. (b) | 9. (b) | 10. (d) |

II

| 1. (a) | 2. (b) | 3. (d) | 4. (a) | 5. (a) | 6. (b) | 7. (c) | 8. (d) | 9. (b) | 10. (a) |
| 11. (d) | 12. (a) | | | | | | | | |

III

| 1. (a) | 2. (c) | 3. (a) | 4. (b) | 5. (a) | 6. (b) | 7. (d) | 8. (b) | 9. (a) |

HOTS

I

| 1. (a) | 2. (b) | 3. (a) | 4. (c) | 5. (a) |

II

| 1. (c) | 2. (b) | 3. (d) | 4. (a) | 5. (c) |

7. PREPOSITION

Answer Key

I

| 1. (d) | 2. (a) | 3. (b) | 4. (a) | 5. (d) | 6. (b) | 7. (a) | 8. (a) | 9. (b) | 10. (c) |
| 11. (a) | 12. (d) | 13. (b) | 14. (c) | 15. (b) | 16. (d) | 17. (c) | 18. (b) | 19. (d) | 20. (a) |

II

| 1. (a) | 2. (c) | 3. (d) | 4. (b) | 5. (a) | 6. (d) | 7. (b) | 8. (c) | 9. (c) | 10. (a) |

HOTS

I

| 1. (c) | 2. (c) | 3. (b) | 4. (a) | 5. (a) |

II

| 1. (a) | 2. (c) | 3. (a) | 4. (c) | 5. (b) |

8. CONJUNCTION

Answer Key

I

| 1. (d) | 2. (a) | 3. (c) | 4. (b) | 5. (d) | 6. (a) | 7. (a) | 8. (c) | 9. (b) | 10. (d) |

II

| 1. (a) | 2. (b) | 3. (b) | 4. (c) | 5. (b) | 6. (a) | 7. (b) | 8. (c) | 9. (a) | 10. (b) |

HOTS

| 1. (a) | 2. (c) | 3. (a) | 4. (b) | 5. (d) | 6. (c) | 7. (d) | 8. (a) | 9. (c) | 10. (b) |

9. PHRASAL VERBS

Answer Key

I

1. (a)	2. (b)	3. (d)	4. (b)	5. (c)	6. (a)	7. (d)	8. (d)	9. (b)	10. (a)
11. (c)	12. (b)	13. (c)	14. (a)	15. (b)					

II

1. (a)	2. (c)	3. (d)	4. (b)	5. (b)	6. (a)	7. (c)	8. (b)	9. (a)	10. (d)
11. (b)	12. (c)	13. (d)	14. (b)	15. (a)					

HOTS

1. (i) make out, (ii) came across, (iii) turn up, (iv) called off.
2. (i) takes after, (ii) sets in, (iii) breaks up, (iv) brought out.
3. (i) bear with, (ii) kept on, (ii) takes after, (iv) passed away.
4. (i) come round, (ii) ran after, (ii) give up, (iv) broke into.
5. (i) gave in, (ii) turned down, (iii) get over, (iv) put up with.

10. PUNCTUATION

Answer Key

I

1. (b)	2. (b)	3. (a)	4. (c)	5. (d)	6. (c)	7. (a)	8. (b)	9. (a)	10. (b)
11. (d)	12. (d)	13. (a)	14. (b)	15. (d)	16. (a)	17. (c)	18. (d)	19. (b)	20. (b)
21. (a)	22. (a)	23. (c)	24. (d)	25. (a)					

HOTS

1. The lady is wearing golden stretch pants, green eyelids and a hives shaped wig.
2. The lady will dress up to go shopping, water the plants, empty the dustbin, answer the phone, read a book and get the letter from the box.
3. Your father has five items in his bathroom – a toothbrush, shaving cream, a razor, a bar of soap and a towel.
4. Hurling has been the national sport of Ireland.
5. We wrote the homonyms too, to see sea in our notebooks.

11. TENSE

Answer Key

I

| 1. (d) | 2. (c) | 3. (b) | 4. (a) | 5. (d) | | | | | |

II

| 1. (b) | 2. (a) | 3. (c) | 4. (d) | 5. (c) | | | | | |

III

| 1. (b) | 2. (c) | 3. (a) | 4. (a) | 5. (d) | | | | | |

IV

| 1. (a) | 2. (b) | 3. (c) | 4. (b) | 5. (d) | 6. (c) | 7. (b) | 8. (a) | 9. (a) | 10. (d) |

V

| 1. (b) | 2. (c) | 3. (a) | 4. (d) | 5. (b) | | | | | |

HOTS

I.
1. Vishal was not living in Kolkata in July last year.
2. Vimal was not talking to Vijay at ten o'clock last night.
3. At four o'clock yesterday we all were not drinking tea.
4. I was not trying to get a taxi at ten o'clock last night.
5. It was not raining in Chennai at five o'clock last evening.

II.
1. Were they crying there?
2. Was he playing cricket?
3. What was he doing?
4. Were Ruchi and Rubi cooking in the kitchen?
5. Where are you both going?

12. VOICE

Answer Key

I

| 1. (a) | 2. (a) | 3. (a) | 4. (b) | 5. (c) | 6. (a) | 7. (c) | 8. (b) | 9. (a) | 10. (b) |
| 11. (a) | 12. (b) | 13. (c) | 14. (a) | 15. (b) | | | | | |

				II					
1. (a)	2. (b)	3. (b)	4. (b)	5. (a)	6. (c)	7. (b)	8. (b)	9. (b)	10. (c)
11. (a)	12. (b)	13. (a)	14. (b)	15. (b)					

HOTS

I				
1. (d)	2. (c)	3. (a)	4. (c)	5. (a)

II				
1. (d)	2. (a)	3. (c)	4. (d)	5. (b)

13. NARRATION

Answer Key

				I					
1. (d)	2. (a)	3. (b)	4. (c)	5. (a)	6. (c)	7. (d)	8. (d)	9. (a)	10. (b)

				II					
1. (a)	2. (b)	3. (d)	4. (a)	5. (b)	6. (a)	7. (b)	8. (c)	9. (a)	10. (d)

HOTS

I				
1. (a)	2. (a)	3. (d)	4. (a)	5. (b)

14. SPELLINGS

Answer Key

I

1. (a)	2. (c)	3. (b)	4. (d)	5. (c)	6. (a)	7. (b)	8. (d)	9. (b)	10. (c)
11. (a)	12. (d)	13. (c)	14. (b)	15. (d)					

II

1. (b)	2. (c)	3. (a)	4. (b)	5. (c)	6. (c)	7. (d)	8. (a)	9. (b)	10. (d)
11. (a)	12. (d)	13. (a)	14. (c)	15. (c)					

HOTS

1. (a)	2. (c)	3. (a)	4. (a)	5. (b)

15. COLLOCATIONS

Answer Key

1. (a)	2. (b)	3. (a)	4. (c)	5. (b)	6. (d)	7. (a)	8. (a)	9. (d)	10. (b)
11. (c)	12. (b)	13. (b)	14. (a)	15. (b)	16. (a)	17. (c)	18. (b)	19. (d)	20. (b)

HOTS

1. (a)	2. (d)	3. (d)	4. (c)	5. (a)

16. IDIOMS

Answer Key

I

1. (a)	2. (b)	3. (c)	4. (a)	5. (d)	6. (b)	7. (c)	8. (b)	9. (c)	10. (d)
11. (a)	12. (a)	13. (b)	14. (c)	15. (d)					

II									
1. (b)	2. (a)	3. (c)	4. (d)	5. (a)	6. (b)	7. (c)	8. (d)	9. (b)	10. (c)

HOTS

1. (c)	2. (b)	3. (b)	4. (d)	5. (a)

17. VOCABULARY

Answer Key

I				
1. (a)	2. (c)	3. (b)	4. (a)	5. (d)

II				
1. (a)	2. (d)	3. (b)	4. (c)	5. (a)

III				
1. (a)	2. (c)	3. (b)	4. (d)	5. (a)

IV				
1. (b)	2. (a)	3. (c)	4. (a)	5. (d)

HOTS

I				
1. (d)	2. (d)	3. (c)	4. (c)	5. (a)

II				
1. (c)	2. (c)	3. (a)	4. (b)	5. (d)

SECTION 2: READING COMPREHENSION

TIPS ON READING COMPREHENSION

Answer Key

I

| 1. (c) | 2. (b) | 3. (a) | 4. (a) | 5. (b) | |

II

| 1. (i) (a) | (ii) (b) | 2. (i) (a) | (ii) (c) | 3. (i) (b) | (ii) (d) |

III

| 1. (b) | 2. (b) | 3. (c) | 4. (b) | 5. (c) |

IV

| 1. (b) | 2. (c) | 3. (a) | 4. (d) | 5. (b) |

V

| 1. (a) | 2. (d) | 3. (c) | 4. (c) | 5. (b) |

VI

| 1. (a) | 2. (d) | 3. (c) | 4. (b) | 5. (b) |

VII

| 1. (a) | 2. (c) | 3. (c) | 4. (c) | 5. (d) |

VIII

| 1. (c) | 2. (a) | 3. (a) | 4. (a) | 5. (d) |

IX

| 1. (a) | 2. (c) | 3. (c) | 4. (d) | 5. (c) |

X				
1. (b)	2. (c)	3. (a)	4. (c)	5. (d)
XI				
1. (c)	2. (b)	3. (c)	4. (a)	5. (c)
XII				
1. (a)	2. (c)	3. (b)	4. (d)	5. (c)

XIII						
1. (b)	2. (a)	3. (c)	4. (d)	5. (b)	6. (a)	7. (d)
XIV						
1. (a)	2. (b)	3. (c)	4. (a)	5. (d)	6. (b)	
XV						
1. (b)	2. (c)	3. (a)	4. (a)	5. (a)		
XVI						
1. (b)	2. (c)	3. (b)	4. (d)	5. (a)		
XVII						
1. (a)	2. (d)	3. (c)	4. (b)	5. (a)	6. (c)	

HOTS				
1. (c)	2. (a)	3. (d)	4. (b)	5. (a)

SECTION 3: SPOKEN AND WRITTEN EXPRESSION

AGREEMENT AND DISAGREEMENT, REQUESTS AND REFUSALS

Answer Key

I

1. (d)	2. (a)	3. (b)	4. (c)	5. (b)	6. (a)	7. (c)	8. (d)	9. (b)	10. (a)
11. (a)	12. (b)	13. (a)	14. (a)	15. (b)					

II

(i) 1. You are absolutely right. 2. Exactly 3. I completely agree. (ii) 1. Are you serious? 2. I do not think so.	(iii) 1. That's a great idea. 2. I have different thoughts on that. (iv) 1. Can you. 2. I'm sorry but that's not possible. (v) 1. Would you mind 2. No way

HOTS

1. (a)	2. (a)	3. (c)	4. (c)	5. (d)

MODEL TEST PAPER – 1

Answer Key

I

1. (d)	2. (d)	3. (a)	4. (d)	5. (d)

II

1. (b)	2. (c)	3. (c)	4. (d)	5. (c)

III

1. (a)	2. (b)	3. (d)	4. (b)	5. (a)

IV				
1. (a)	2. (b)	3. (c)	4. (a)	5. (c)
V				
1. (d)	2. (a)	3. (b)	4. (b)	5. (c)
VI				
1. (b)	2. (a)	3. (c)	4. (b)	5. (d)
VII				
1. (a)	2. (d)	3. (b)	4. (b)	5. (c)
VIII				
1. (b)	2. (b)	3. (c)	4. (a)	5. (d)
IX				
1. (b)	2. (c)	3. (d)		
4. The game of cricket is very popular in India.				
5. (a) Horse racing 5. (b) Polo				
X				
1. (a)	2. (b)	3. (b)	4. (a)	5. (b)

MODEL TEST PAPER – 2

Answer Key

1. (c)	2. (d)	3. (b)	4. (c)	5. (a)	6. (b)	7. (d)	8. (b)	9. (c)	10. (a)
11. (c)	12. (b)	13. (a)	14. (d)	15. (c)	16. (b)	17. (a)	18. (d)	19. (a)	20. (c)
21. (b)	22. (c)	23. (d)	24. (b)	25. (a)	26. (d)	27. (a)	28. (c)	29. (b)	30. (d)
31. (b)	32. (b)	33. (b)	34. (c)	35. (a)	36. (c)	37. (c)	38. (d)	39. (b)	40. (a)
41. (b)	42. (a)	43. (c)	44. (d)	45. (c)	46. (a)	47. (b)	48. (d)	49. (c)	50. (a)

Appendix

There are different organizations that conduct these examinations and covering all of them is not needed as the focus should be to understand the main type of exams conducted. They are similar for these organizations with the difference being the change in name of the exam.

Science Olympiad Foundation (SOF)		
S. No.	Name of Exam	Grade
1.	National Science Olympiad (NSO)	Class 1-10
2.	National Cyber Olympiad (NCO)	Class 1-10
3.	International Mathematics Olympiad (IMO)	Class 1-10
4.	International English Olympiad (IEO)	Class 1-10
5.	International Commerce Olympiad (ICO)	Class 1-10
6.	International General Knowledge Olympiad (IGKO)	Class 1-10
7.	International Social Studies Olympiad (ISSO)	Class 1-10

Indian Talent Olympiad (ITO)		
S. No.	Name of Exam	Grade
1.	International Science Olympiad (ISO)	Class 1-12
2.	International Math Olympiad (IMO)	Class 1-12
3.	English International Olympiad (EIO)	Class 1-12
4.	General Knowledge International Olympiad (GKIO)	Class 1-12
5.	International Computer Olympiad (ICO)	Class 1-12
6.	International Drawing Olympiad (IDO)	Class 1-12
7.	National Essay Olympiad (NESO)	Class 1-12
8.	National Social Studies Olympiad (NSSO)	Class 1-12

EduHeal Foundation		
S. No.	Name of Exam	Grade
1.	Eduheal International Cyber Olympiad (ICO)	Class 1-12
2.	Eduheal International English Olympiad (IEO)	Class 1-12
3.	National Interactive Math Olympiad (NIMO)	Class 1-12
4.	National Interactive Science Olympiad (NISO)	Class 1-12
5.	International General Knowledge Olympiad (IGO)	Class 1-12
6.	National Space Science Olympiad (NSSO)	Class 1-12

S. No.	Humming Bird Education	
	Name of Exam	Grade
1.	Humming Bird Commerce Competency Olympiad (HCC)	Class 1-12
2.	Humming Bird Cyber Olympiad (HCO)	Class 1-12
3.	Humming Bird English Olympiad (HEO)	Class 1-12
4.	Humming Bird General Knowledge Olympiad (HGO)	Class 1-12
5.	Humming Bird Hindi Olympiad (HHO)	Class 1-12
6.	Humming Bird Mathematics Olympiad (HMO)	Class 1-12
7.	Humming Bird Science Olympiad (HSO)	Class 1-12
8.	Humming Bird Aptitude and Reasoning Olympiad (ARO)	Class 1-12
9.	Humming Bird Spelling Competition (Spell BEE)	Class 1-12
10.	Humming Bird Language Olympiad	Class 1-12

S. No.	International Assessments for Indian Schools (IAIS) (MacMillan and EEA Collaboration)	
	Name of Exam	Grade
1.	IAIS Maths Olympiad	Class 3-12
2.	IAIS ScienceOlympiad	Class 3-12
3.	IAIS English Olympiad	Class 3-12
4.	IAIS Digital Technologies Olympiad	Class 3-12

S. No.	SilverZone Foundation	
	Name of Exam	Grade
1.	International Informatics Olympiad	Class 1-12
2.	International Olympiad of Mathematics	Class 1-12
3.	International Olympiad of Science	Class 1-12

S. No.	Unified Council	
	Name of Exam	Grade
1.	Unified Council Cyber Exam	Class 1-12
2.	Unified International English Olympiad.	Class 1-12
3.	Unified International Mathematics Olympiad (UIMO)	Class 1-12

S. No.	Unicus	
	Name of Exam	Grade
1.	Unicus Non-Routine Mathematics Olympiad (UNRMO)	Class 1-11
2.	Unicus Mathematics Olympiad (UMO)	Class 1-11

3.	Unicus Science Olympiad (USO)	Class 1-11
4.	Unicus English Olympiad (UEO)	Class 1-11
5.	Unicus Cyber Olympiad (UCO)	Class 1-11
6.	Unicus General knowledge Olympiad (UGKO)	Class 1-11
7.	Unicus Critical Thinking Olympiad (UCTO)	Class 1-11
	CREST (Online Mode)	
S. No.	**Name of Exam**	**Grade**
1.	Mathematics (CMO)	Classes KG-10
2.	Science (CSO)	Classes KG-10
3.	English (CEO)	Classes KG-10
4.	Computer (CCO)	Classes 1-10
5.	Reasoning (CRO)	Classes 1-10
6.	Spell Bee Summer (CSB)	Classes 1-8
7.	Spell Bee Winter (CSBW)	Classes 1-8
8.	Mental Maths (MMO)	Classes 1-12
9.	Green Warrior Olympiad (GWO)	Classes 1-12

How To Apply?

Anyone willing to participate in the Olympiad exam can follow these steps to apply for the exam:

- ☞ Log in to the official website of the conducting organization.
- ☞ Find the Registration Option to register
- ☞ Fill up the details such as Student Name, Parent Name, School Name, Class, Postal Address, E-mail Address, Password, etc.
- ☞ Select the subjects you want to apply for. Pay the necessary registration fees and you are done.
- ☞ You will receive necessary details on your email id.

There are no minimum marks required by the Olympiad conducting organizations to apply for the exam.

Awards

Based on the organization rules, students as well as schools participating in these exams are awarded with several recognitions based on the marks they score.

www.ingramcontent.com/pod-product-compliance
Lightning Source LLC
Chambersburg PA
CBHW080343170426
43194CB00014B/2669